W9-BZR-697

DORLING KINDERSLEY 📖 EYEWITNESS BOOKS

BUILDING

18th century carved
and stippled staircase
tread end

Dutch
Delftware tile

Porcelain tile made in China
during the Han Dynasty

Wrought-iron
baluster

Octagonal tower
of the Château de
Chamerolles, France

Gabled town house,
Lemgo, Germany

Part of a
Mesopotamian brick
course, 6th century B.C.

Medieval gargoyle
of man with flat cap

Medieval gargoyle of
monk wearing a cowl

DK EYEWITNESS BOOKS

BUILDING

Written by
PHILIP WILKINSON

Photographed by
DAVE KING & GEOFF DANN

Crown post used
as a roof support

Victorian fanlight

16th-century wrought-
iron casement window

DK
Dorling Kindersley

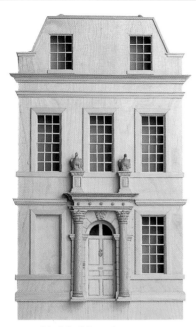

Model of Georgian town house, Bath, England

Tiles laid in a fish-scale pattern

18th-century wooden architrave

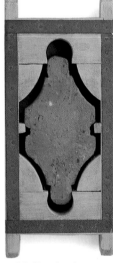

Dorling Kindersley
LONDON, NEW YORK, AUCKLAND, DELHI, JOHANNESBURG, MUNICH,
PARIS and SYDNEY

For a full catalog, visit

DK www.dk.com

Project editor Miranda Smith
Art editor Manisha Patel
Editor Djinn von Noorden
Managing editor Simon Adams
Managing art editor Julia Harris
Researcher Céline Carez
Production Catherine Semark
Picture research Cynthia Hole

This Eyewitness ® Book has been conceived by
Dorling Kindersley Limited and Editions Gallimard

Published in the United States by
Dorling Kindersley Publishing, Inc.
375 Hudson Street,
New York, NY 10014
4 6 8 10 9 7 5

Dorling Kindersley books are available at special discounts for bulk purchases for sales promotions
or premiums. Special editions, including personalized covers, excerpts of existing guides, and
corporate imprints can be created in large quantities for specific needs. For more information,
contact Special Markets Dept., Dorling Kindersley Publishing, Inc., 95 Madison Ave., New York,
NY 10016; Fax: (800) 600-9098

Library of Congress Cataloging-in-Publication Data
Wilkinson, Philip.
Building / written by Philip Wilkinson;
photographed by Dave King & Geoff Dann.
p. cm. — (Eyewitness Books) Includes index.
1. Structural engineering—Juvenile literature. 2. House
construction—Juvenile literature. 3. Building materials—Juvenile literature
[1. Structural engineering. 2. House construction. 3. Building materials.]
I. King, Dave, ill. II. Dann, Geoff, ill. III. Title. IV. Series.
TA634.W54 2000   690—dc20
ISBN 0-7894-6027-0 (pb)
ISBN 0-7894-6026-2 (hc)

Color reproduction by Colourscan, Singapore
Printed in China by Toppan Printing Co. (Shenzhen) Ltd.

Traditional tin-glazed earthenware Delft tile

Detail from medieval stained glass window, Canterbury Cathedral, England

Mullion brick in its wooden mold

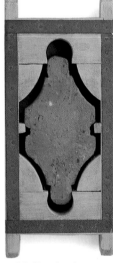

Cross-section of an oak tree trunk

Contents

Jettied timber-framed houses, England

What is a building?

THE VERY SIMPLEST BUILDING is a permanent structure with a roof and four walls. Houses, schools, factories, and business offices are all buildings. So are stables and pigsties. A building is shaped partly by its purpose – a farmhouse looks very different from, for example, a ski chalet. A building is also shaped by the technology available to construct it, the constraints of the site, the history of the type of building, and the materials at hand. Wood, stone, and brick are three common traditional building materials. Modern buildings may also be made of steel, concrete, and glass. But most buildings provide people with more than just shelter from the weather. Making buildings beautiful with ornament or extensions is important, because it makes people feel good. And because building styles change over the years, people find the development of building and architecture a useful way of looking at the past.

PEOPLE POWER
Building often involves materials that are heavy. Skilled workers, such as these medieval stone masons, are needed to handle them. In the Middle Ages machines such as this treadmill for hauling stones up the side of a tower, were powered by people. Today, electrically powered machines are used to do all the heavy work.

Elevation of a late-19th-century house

Section through the same house

THE BEST-LAID PLANS
An architect usually makes drawings before any construction begins. An elevation shows the building from one side, while a section shows parts of the buildings that are not usually visible, such as roof beams and floor joists. The architect also makes a set of floor plans for the builder to follow. These must be to scale, and show measurements and details of the structure.

ROWS AND ROWS
Earth – usually in the form of bricks – has always been used to make buildings. Red is the most common color for bricks in the western world, though many other shades can be made. The colour varies according to the local clay. After the industrial revolution of the 18th and 19th centuries, bricks were manufactured on a much larger scale than before. Rows of red-brick houses, such as these in New York, were built in the thousands.

Walls are made of wooden planks joined together

Overhanging roof keeps rain and snow off walls

Wooden balcony

ALL IN WOOD
Nearly every house contains some wood, but in places where trees are plentiful, buildings are often made completely of timber. Wood has the advantage over brick and stone of being lighter and easier to cut and work. In the right climate, or protected with an overhanging roof like this chalet in the Austrian Alps, wooden houses can last for hundreds of years. But there is a high fire risk, so wooden houses often have brick or stone chimneys.

TEAMWORK

Most buildings are put together by a large team of people, from the architects who design the structure, to laborers who clear the site and carry the materials. Other specialist workers may include bricklayers to build the walls, carpenters to make wooden fittings, and plumbers to lay the pipes for the plumbing. The men in this picture are roofers, fixing on wooden battens before laying tiles.

LOCAL MATERIALS

Builders in rural areas often use whatever materials they can find nearby. This might be palm leaves in Southeast Asia, wood in Scandinavia, or as here, reeds in South America. Making huts like these requires traditional skills, which in many communities are still handed down from one generation to the other.

FUTURE HOUSE

Modern houses are becoming more energy-efficient, with better insulation and features such as glazed roofs to trap the heat of the sun. In some places, solar panels may be used to generate power from the sun's rays. In addition, materials that do not take too much energy to make are being more widely used.

HOUSE OF STONE

This ornate house by the Grand Canal in Venice shows how well stone can be adapted for a highly decorated building. Some of the statues were originally gilded, giving the house its name of Ca' d'Oro, or House of Gold. As well as providing a decorative effect, most building stones are strong and long-lasting. Patterns are made with different facing stones and the house adorned with carvings.

Intricate stone tracery

Stone finial

Traces of gilt decoration

Stone facing

Stone balcony

Building with wood

MOST BUILDINGS CONTAIN some wood. Wood is often used to make doors or the beams that hold up the roof. A whole building may be made of wood. The first builders used whatever type of wood they could find nearby, but they soon learned that some trees were better for particular building tasks than others. Hardwoods, from trees such as oak and elm were highly prized. Today, softwoods, from conifers (cone-bearing trees), are often used. Early carpenters devised a series of joints to attach the timbers to one another. Some of those are still used today. The tools medieval carpenters used to form these joints have also changed remarkably little.

Unplaned oak

Planed oak

OAK
Oak, the most popular wood for building in western Europe, is a close-grained hardwood. It is ideal for structural timbers such as wall posts and rafters. Oak beams are heavy and large ones are difficult to lift into place; once in position, they last for centuries.

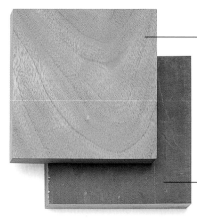

Strong wood with a beautiful grain

Unplaned mahogany

MAHOGANY
In its native tropical areas of Africa, South America, and the Far East, mahogany was a traditional building wood. However, since the 1500s, it has been exported in large quantities to Europe, and now the wild mahogany forests are seriously depleted.

A tough wood with conspicuous growth rings

Unplaned larch

LARCH
Softwoods such as larch, that are quick-growing and inexpensive have been used for many centuries in their native northern areas. Nowadays, conifers are grown commercially in many parts of the world; they are often used for floorboards, doors, and windowframes.

Bark will be trimmed off at a later stage

Wood is sliced into boards by giant band saw

Leftover pieces of wood are used for chipboard or pulp for paper making

Grain direction varies from board to board

THROUGH-AND-THROUGH SAWING
There are many ways of turning a log into planks or beams. Today, various methods are used, but through-and-through sawing, which slices through the wood in one direction, is popular for cheaper types of wood. The method is simple and produces many planks, and very little of the wood is wasted. However, the way the grain is cut makes the boards likely to warp. The most ancient method of cutting up a log was simply to remove the outer material to make a single rectangular section. This is known as a boxed heart. If the tree was large enough, this section could be sawed down the middle to make two beams.

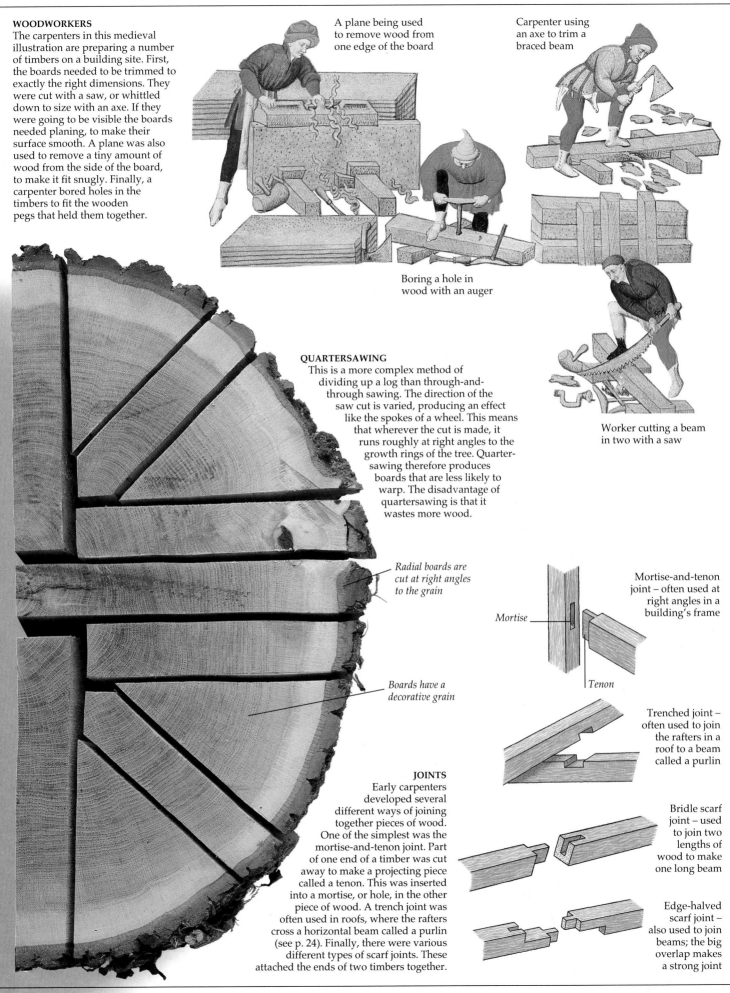

WOODWORKERS

The carpenters in this medieval illustration are preparing a number of timbers on a building site. First, the boards needed to be trimmed to exactly the right dimensions. They were cut with a saw, or whittled down to size with an axe. If they were going to be visible the boards needed planing, to make their surface smooth. A plane was also used to remove a tiny amount of wood from the side of the board, to make it fit snugly. Finally, a carpenter bored holes in the timbers to fit the wooden pegs that held them together.

A plane being used to remove wood from one edge of the board

Carpenter using an axe to trim a braced beam

Boring a hole in wood with an auger

Worker cutting a beam in two with a saw

QUARTERSAWING

This is a more complex method of dividing up a log than through-and-through sawing. The direction of the saw cut is varied, producing an effect like the spokes of a wheel. This means that wherever the cut is made, it runs roughly at right angles to the growth rings of the tree. Quartersawing therefore produces boards that are less likely to warp. The disadvantage of quartersawing is that it wastes more wood.

Radial boards are cut at right angles to the grain

Boards have a decorative grain

Mortise

Tenon

Mortise-and-tenon joint – often used at right angles in a building's frame

Trenched joint – often used to join the rafters in a roof to a beam called a purlin

Bridle scarf joint – used to join two lengths of wood to make one long beam

Edge-halved scarf joint – also used to join beams; the big overlap makes a strong joint

JOINTS

Early carpenters developed several different ways of joining together pieces of wood. One of the simplest was the mortise-and-tenon joint. Part of one end of a timber was cut away to make a projecting piece called a tenon. This was inserted into a mortise, or hole, in the other piece of wood. A trench joint was often used in roofs, where the rafters cross a horizontal beam called a purlin (see p. 24). Finally, there were various different types of scarf joints. These attached the ends of two timbers together.

Wooden houses

Wood is one of the most versatile building materials. Where trees are plentiful, the complete structure may be made of wood, as with the traditional Scandinavian log cabin. Alternatively, the house may be based on a wood framework, such as the ancient cruck- or timber-framed designs in Europe, and the wooden frame houses of North America. Yet another use of wood is as siding on outside walls, as seen on many clapboarded houses in the U.S. Even the shape of a piece of wood may determine its function – tree trunks, for example, make good pillars.

IN THE FRAME
Frame houses are a common type of construction in the U.S. They are built on a wooden frame, and sided with wood clapboards on the outside. The sidings can be left bare, or covered with more decorative material such as stucco (outside plasterwork). On the old Paul Revere House in Boston, Massachusetts, the wood sidings can be seen clearly. Shingles on the roof complete a house made almost entirely of wood.

BOARDED UP
Horizontal boards, called clapboard siding, or weatherboarding, cover the sides of this house in Williamsburg, Virginia. The technique gives extra protection against the elements, and makes the interior warmer.

CRUCK FRAME
This is the simplest wooden frame. Shaped like an inverted V, the cruck frame consists of two timbers made from the same tree trunk, so that they match exactly. These timbers are visible at both ends of this typical cruck-framed building.

Turf roof to withstand adverse weather

Protective covering on top of chimney keeps out snow and nesting birds

Wall made of tree trunks, trimmed to make a flat surface

WOODEN BARN
Farm buildings such as this traditional barn near Oslo, Norway, are often made of wood. This barn is raised on wooden pillars, and the sides are cut in an elegant pattern. These holes ensure good ventilation, and the pillars and overhanging roof keep out the damp and help prevent pests from eating the contents.

WALLS OF PAPER
Wood was once a common building material in Japan. Traditional buildings have wooden frames, and roofs with a large overhang. The gaps between the framework are sometimes filled with movable screens covered in paper. These screens diffuse the strong summer sun.

HOUSE ON STILTS
Tropical houses are often raised above the ground on wooden stilts. This is usually to keep the building and its occupants well clear of the damp during the rainy season. It also helps to keep out pests such as snakes. This raised building is a traditional long house in Sarawak, Borneo.

Carved wooden barge board conceals ends of rafters

Shutters with wooden latticework design

LIFE IN A LOG CABIN
Scandinavia and Russia, with their abundant pine forests, are the places to find traditional log cabins. The logs are split, cut smooth with an axe, and grooved at the ends so that they fit together snugly at the corners. This cabin, which is unusual because of its elaborately carved exterior, was built near Moscow in Russia.

Ornate tympanum (arch above doorway) is carved with date of construction

Notches where logs join at end of bay

LOG FARMHOUSE
Scandinavian log houses, such as this farmhouse, are sometimes quite large. It was not always possible to find long enough logs to stretch the entire length of the house, so the walls had to be made in several units, or bays. A roof of grassy turf planted on pine planks provided a tough, windproof covering.

Shutters keep house wind- and rainproof in winter

Stone plinth ensures that house is level and free from rising damp

Earth and all its uses

Eᴀʀᴛʜ ᴄᴀɴ ʙᴇ ᴜꜱᴇᴅ in two main ways in building: unbaked, as mud, or as bricks, baked in the sun or in a kiln. To build a wall with unbaked earth, the mud usually needs to be mixed with chopped straw, a little lime to bind it together, and some sand or gravel to give it strength. Then the wall can be built up in courses, or layers, while the mud is still wet. Alternatively, a dry mud mix can be pushed between boards to form a wall, a technique known as *pisé*. Today, the most common use of earth is to make bricks. They are strong, durable, and much lighter than either mud or stone. Bricks can also be made in a uniform size, making it easy to lay them in courses. Since the time of the ancient Middle Eastern civilizations, they have been widely popular.

BANKING ON EARTH
One of the simplest uses of earth is to build a bank. Banks can be used for fortification, as at the ancient Maiden Castle in southern England. The banks and ditches were built as a deterrent to enemies, who would also have had to scale a wooden fence around the topmost rampart. On a smaller scale, banks can help to support structures of other materials, as with the houses at Skara Brae, Orkney (see p. 16).

ANCIENT CONCRETE
The Romans used a volcanic earth called pozzolana, mixing it with materials such as brick and stone rubble to make an early form of concrete. They used this material to build vaults, arches, and ovens like these at Pompeii.

PALACE OF BRICKS
The Caliph Al Mu'tasim built this palace of sun-dried bricks at Samara, Iraq, in the 9th century A.D. The throne room was most magnificent; it had a tall vaulted ceiling made of bricks.

BEEHIVE HOUSES
Parts of Syria were well known for ancient mud houses in the shape of beehives. Most of these houses were made by building up layers of wet mud, and letting each layer dry before adding another. Toward the top, the layers were wound tighter, to make the tapering roof. When the structure was finished, the whole thing was given a smooth finish with mud plaster.

Part of a Mesopotamian brick course, 6th century B.C.

Adobe wall decorated with traditional earth colors

Overhanging thatched roof of local straw

Ropes secure thatch firmly to roof

A GOOD HAT
This house (right) was built in the style of the ancient iron-age buildings of Britain. A pit was dug and a low mud wall built. Straw and animal hair were mixed in with the mud to help bind it together. Because this material is vulnerable to the damp, the thatched roof was made with a wide overhang – builders used to say that a mud wall needed "a good hat."

Porch shelters doorway from prevailing wind

DESERT HOUSES
In dry, sunny places all over the world, clay buildings are still constructed with adobe – mud made into blocks and dried in the sun. An adobe house is fast and easy to build, and in rural villages all the men help when a new one is needed. In Rajasthan, India, houses like those in the picture above are sometimes so brightly decorated with traditional designs that it is difficult to see the joints between the blocks.

Manufacturing mud bricks in a wooden mold, Kano, Nigeria

Mud bricks being used to build a house near the Jos Plateau, Nigeria

Brickmaking
Clay has been used to make bricks for at least 6,000 years. At first, the wet mud was shaped in a bottomless wooden mold. The mold was removed and the brick was left to dry in the sun. But soon people applied the knowledge gained in making pottery and began to fire bricks in a kiln. The high temperature and the use of glazes meant that the bricks could be made resistant to water.

Firing bricks in a kiln at Luxor in Egypt

GLAZED OVER
Some of the finest early bricks come from Mesopotamia, the area of modern Iraq where the Middle East's first great cities grew up. Sometimes these bricks were made in pattern molds, so that an elegant design could be built up as the bricks were laid. The bricks were cemented together by a mix of mud and water which dried in the sun. These bricks, from a temple of the 6th century B.C., were also glazed and fired in a kiln in order to make them waterproof.

Striking pattern would have stood out on external wall of a temple

13

Building with bricks

BRICKS ARE STRONG, long-lasting, and easy to manufacture in bulk. They are usually made in standard sizes, which makes them simpler to work with than irregular blocks of stone. As well as being functional, bricks can be attractive when part of a wall, since their appearance varies according to their color and the bonds, or patterns, in which they are laid. Bricks were often made near a building site – clay was dug from a pit and kneaded in a device called a pug mill until it reached the right consistency. The clay was then put into wooden moulds, and the bricks were heated in a kiln until they were rock-hard. When the industrial revolution led to a massive demand for cheaply built factories and houses in the 19th century, bricks began to be made on a larger scale, and were transported from the brickworks to the building site.

Wooden cross-braces

FILLING IN THE GAPS
Some wood-framed buildings have panels of brick between the timbers. Because bricks are heavier than material such as wattle and daub (see pp. 20-21), the wooden beams and posts have to be strong to support them. Wooden frames with brick infill often sag and subside with time. To avoid this, the builders of this German house have put in extra X-shaped cross braces.

A BRICKLAYER'S BUSINESS
While the bricklayer does the skilled job of fixing the bricks in straight courses, a laborer mixes sand and cement to make mortar. He takes bricks up to the bricklayer, using the hod which is leaning against the wall.

BONDED TOGETHER (below)
Bricks can be laid in many ways, with the ends (headers) and sides (stretchers) arranged in different courses. Today, stretcher bond – with all the stretchers visible – is the most common. But there are other, more attractive arrangements. Header-and-stretcher bond was common in early brick buildings, and Flemish bond became fashionable after the 17th century.

Stretcher bond

Flemish bond

English cross bond
(a header-and-stretcher bond)

Rounded portion to make molding visible from outside the building

Wooden mold

Ornate brick

Groove to take glass

Gap where fired brick has shrunk away from mould

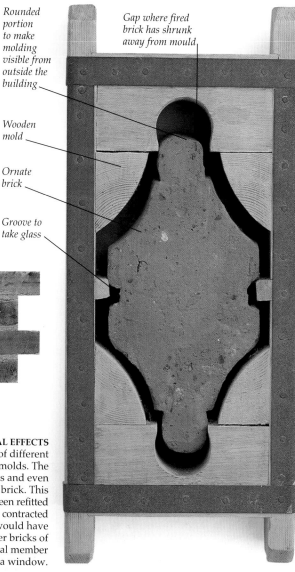

SPECIAL EFFECTS
Bricks can be cast in all sorts of different shapes using special wooden molds. The Romans made scroll patterns and even entire Corinthian capitals in brick. This modern mullion brick has been refitted into its mold to show how it has contracted during the firing process. It would have been used, along with many other bricks of the same design, to form the vertical member between two panes of glass in a window.

HOUSE OF MANY COLORS

Bricks have always varied in color – either because different clays were used, or because of uneven heat in the kiln. Sometimes builders take advantage of this fact by making colored patterns with bricks, an effect known as polychrome. Red, yellow, and gray bricks make bold geometrical patterns on this house.

PAINTED AND DECORATED

Although the original colors of old bricks are often beautiful in their own right, modern mass-produced bricks can be rather harsh to look at. Sometimes the owners of a row of terraced houses solve this problem by painting their homes. When they choose different colors, the result can be pleasing, as with these houses in Washington, D.C.

Triangular pediment of brick is covered in plaster

Hoist to lift furniture into upper room

Brick laid in English cross bond

Plaster decoration hides bricks

DIAMOND PATTERNS

The custom of making polychrome patterns with bricks began in northern France in the 15th century. These examples from the Château de Sully are typical of these early diamond patterns. The colors were not produced during the brickmaking process, however, they were painted on after the bricks were fixed in place.

Brick arch over window to take weight of wall above

AWAY WITH THE CLAY

These tall houses are typical of the city of Amsterdam, in the Netherlands. Clay was easier to come by than stone, so even the richest merchants built their houses from brick. Stone was sometimes used for ornamental details, although these were often made of brick covered in white plaster. Large windows help lessen the weight of the structure of these houses, lessening the load on the city's watery ground, as well as the risk of subsidence (sinking).

Stone and its uses

THE BEST BUILDING STONES are decorative, lend themselves well to ornamental carving, and last for centuries. But stone is heavy to transport, laborious to work, and not always available. In many places, stone is kept for the most prestigious buildings, and stonemasons are the most valued and highly skilled of building workers. There are many types of building stone, from tough granites to soft sandstones, flint nodules to beach pebbles, and all have a distinctive appearance. The way the stone is worked also affects the look of a building. Hard stones like flint are often laid in irregular pieces with wide mortar courses to create a rustic effect. Softer stones like limestone can be dressed finely so that when their flat surfaces are laid together the join is not visible.

THE RIGHT SIZE AND SHAPE
These masons in Yemen are dressing (finishing) rough-hewn blocks of stone to the required shape, and arranging them to form a wall. They have set up a horizontal string to ensure that each individual course is level.

STONE-AGE SETTLEMENT
Building with stone began in places where no other materials were available. On the island of Orkney, in Scotland, Neolithic people built a tiny village called Skara Brae between about 3100 and 2500 B.C. The walls of the houses are made of local stone, protected by banks of earth. Everything in the houses – even the beds – were made of stone.

THE GREAT PYRAMIDS
The Egyptian pyramids were the first large-scale stone monuments. The greatest of them all was built at Giza for King Khufu around 2550 B.C. It is built mainly of blocks of limestone weighing 2.5 tons. The limestone came from nearby, but parts of the interior are made of granite, brought from Aswan 500 miles (800 km) up the River Nile.

Fine-grained matrix

Dark, angular fragments of limestone

LIMESTONE
The gradual build-up of dead sea animals in ancient seas eventually produced limestone, a sedimentary rock. There are many different types, from the pale, soft chalk to the harder, carboniferous limestones. They also vary greatly in color, with impurities such as iron adding tinges of orange to the stone. Softer than granite, limestone is quite easy to carve, but does not survive well in a polluted atmosphere. Many of the ornate details of medieval churches and cathedrals are carved in limestone.

Gray quartz crystals

Feldspar gives a pink coloring

GRANITE
Granite is an igneous rock, formed millions of years ago by intense heat and pressure underground. The resulting stone is extremely hard and difficult to work but virtually indestructible. It is valued where strength is important – for example, the great load-bearing slabs above the main chambers in the Great Pyramid. It is impervious to water and resistant to air pollution, and is ideal for building in cities, and for structures such as lighthouses.

Small, dark patches of carbon

TO EACH HIS TASK
These medieval masons from a 13th-century Irish manuscript are demonstrating some of the skills involved in building with stone. First, the stone needs to be cut to the right size and shape. The worker on the far right is using an axe to shape a long piece of stone – probably a lintel to go over a door. Then the stone has to be carried to the right place – here, a laborer is using a pulley. As the wall is built, a mason has to check that it is perfectly level. Finally, skilled stonecarvers work on the decorative parts of the building.

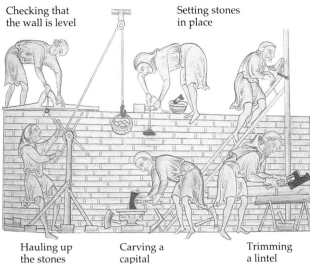
Checking that the wall is level

Setting stones in place

Hauling up the stones

Carving a capital

Trimming a lintel

SLATE
Slate, a metamorphic rock, was formed when existing rocks were changed by intense heat and pressure. It can easily be split into thin sheets and is a perfect roofing material because it is thin, light, and waterproof. Slate has also been used for flooring and for facing the outsides of buildings.

GRAND DESIGNS
In the 18th century, stone was the preferred choice for large buildings. It was ideal for carving classical details such as statues and triangular pediments. And it was the only material in which massive columns, like these on the front of the Villa Pisani at Stra in Italy, could be built.

Small grains of quartz

SANDSTONE
These stones contain crystals of quartz, often surrounded by other materials which can range from very soft to very hard. Sandstones also vary greatly in color, from pink to green. The harder sandstones make good building materials, being more resistant to pollution than limestone, but still relatively easy to work.

MODERN MASONRY (above)
The labor entailed in quarrying and working stone means that today it is more often used in small quantities as a facing material rather than for structural purposes. But for clients who can spend the money, such as the owner of this royal residence in Bahrain, stone is still a good material that can be worked to produce elegant, long-lasting structures.

CUTTING IT TO SIZE
Masons can use a saw to trim large blocks of stone to the right size. These 11th-century Italian workers are using a two-handed saw typical of the Middle Ages to cut a large block of marble.

MARBLE
Prized by the ancient Greeks and Romans, this metamorphic rock is easy to cut and polish, and is found in a variety of beautiful colors and different textures. In the Renaissance, this stone was used on a large scale for building purposes, with whole columns made of marble. In Indian art, different colored marble was often used to create decorative inlays on walls (see p. 60).

Carved in stone

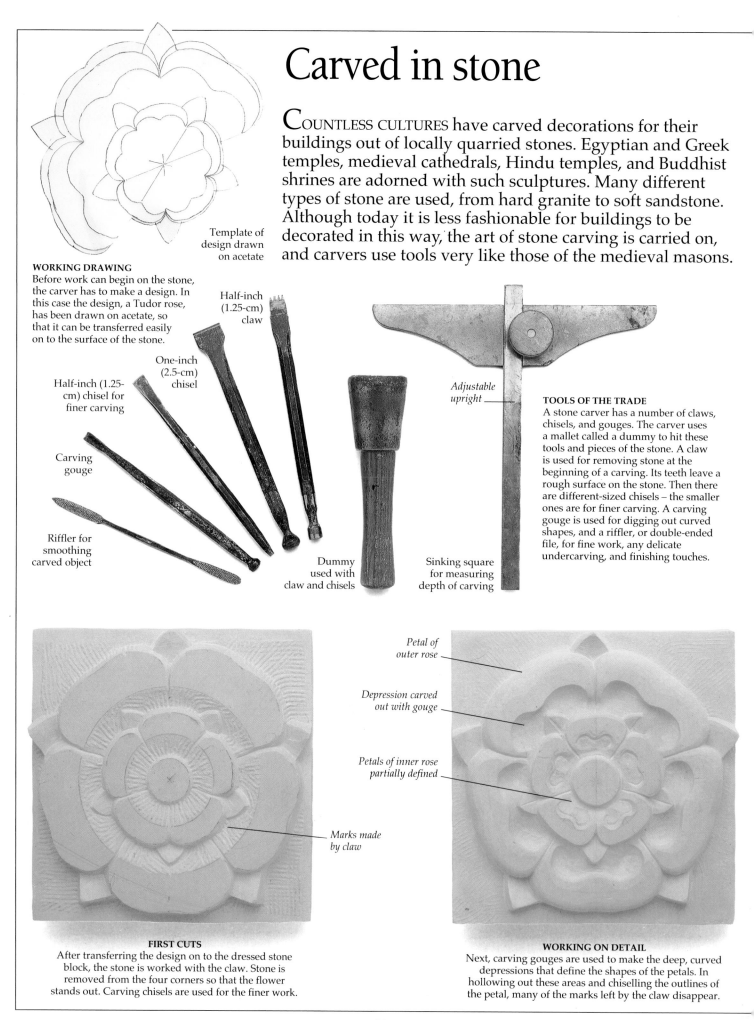

COUNTLESS CULTURES have carved decorations for their buildings out of locally quarried stones. Egyptian and Greek temples, medieval cathedrals, Hindu temples, and Buddhist shrines are adorned with such sculptures. Many different types of stone are used, from hard granite to soft sandstone. Although today it is less fashionable for buildings to be decorated in this way, the art of stone carving is carried on, and carvers use tools very like those of the medieval masons.

Template of design drawn on acetate

WORKING DRAWING
Before work can begin on the stone, the carver has to make a design. In this case the design, a Tudor rose, has been drawn on acetate, so that it can be transferred easily on to the surface of the stone.

Half-inch (1.25-cm) claw

One-inch (2.5-cm) chisel

Half-inch (1.25-cm) chisel for finer carving

Carving gouge

Riffler for smoothing carved object

Dummy used with claw and chisels

Adjustable upright

Sinking square for measuring depth of carving

TOOLS OF THE TRADE
A stone carver has a number of claws, chisels, and gouges. The carver uses a mallet called a dummy to hit these tools and pieces of the stone. A claw is used for removing stone at the beginning of a carving. Its teeth leave a rough surface on the stone. Then there are different-sized chisels – the smaller ones are for finer carving. A carving gouge is used for digging out curved shapes, and a riffler, or double-ended file, for fine work, any delicate undercarving, and finishing touches.

Marks made by claw

FIRST CUTS
After transferring the design on to the dressed stone block, the stone is worked with the claw. Stone is removed from the four corners so that the flower stands out. Carving chisels are used for the finer work.

Petal of outer rose

Depression carved out with gouge

Petals of inner rose partially defined

WORKING ON DETAIL
Next, carving gouges are used to make the deep, curved depressions that define the shapes of the petals. In hollowing out these areas and chiselling the outlines of the petal, many of the marks left by the claw disappear.

MEN AT WORK

This picture of masons and stonecarvers illustrates a 15th-century manuscript by Jean Fouquet. The worker on the left is dressing a stone block – trimming it to a square shape. The carvers on the right are working at various tasks: carving a statue; carving ornamental moldings to go around an arch or doorway; and making a mortice (hole) in the top of a carved stone block, inside which part of another stone will fit.

Dressing a stone block with an axe

Carving a statue with a chisel

Carving moldings with an axe

Cutting a mortice with a chisel

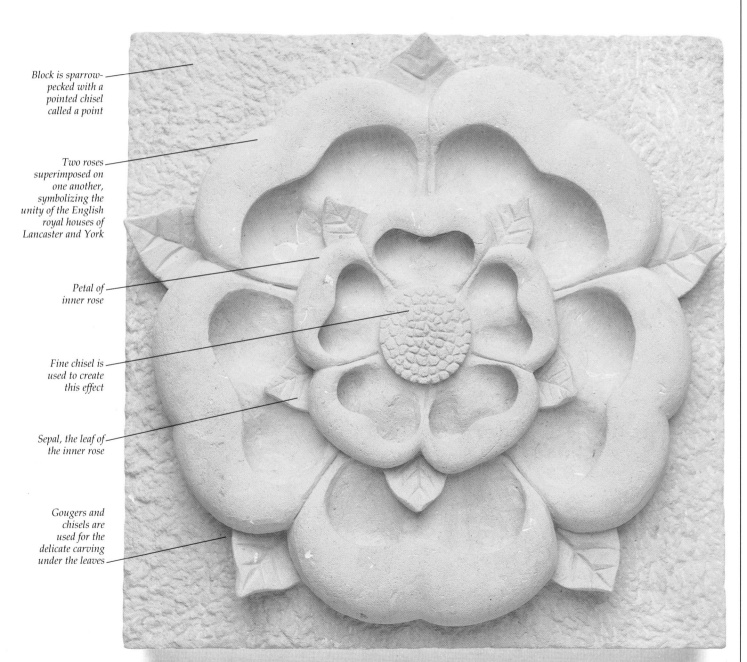

Block is sparrow-pecked with a pointed chisel called a point

Two roses superimposed on one another, symbolizing the unity of the English royal houses of Lancaster and York

Petal of inner rose

Fine chisel is used to create this effect

Sepal, the leaf of the inner rose

Gougers and chisels are used for the delicate carving under the leaves

THE FINISHED TUDOR ROSE

The petals of the inner rose, the sepals, and the center are finished. Finally, the double-ended file called the riffler is used to remove the fine chisel marks. To make the rose stand out from its background, the four corners of the stone are carved to give a rough surface. In medieval buildings, after the carver had finished, the rose was painted.

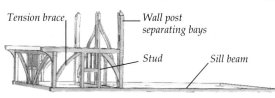

1 FIRST BAY

Tension brace — *Wall post separating bays* — *Stud* — *Sill beam*

The sill beams are placed on stone blocks or a plinth. The uprights of the first bay are assembled – first the wall posts, tall timbers which separate this bay from the next, then the other uprights with their braces, and then the horizontals.

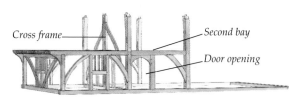

2 SECOND BAY

Cross frame — *Second bay* — *Door opening*

Diagonal braces are added to make a cross frame which ties the two sides of the building together. Then the carpenters start to assemble the second bay. Features such as door frames are built into the structure.

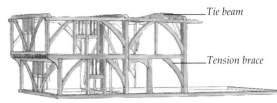

3 UPPER STORY

Tie beam — *Tension brace*

The upper story is assembled. Like the first, it consists of studs and tension braces. This is a jettied building, so wooden brackets help support the overhanging first floor. Floor timbers are built into the first bay, not into the second.

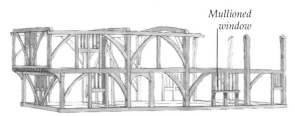

4 THIRD AND FOURTH BAYS

Mullioned window

The mullions (the upright bars of the window) were already built into the structure. When the assembly took place, the upright timbers were supported by temporary timbers, which were removed once the braces and studs were in place.

5 PRINCIPAL RAFTERS

Tie beam — *Principal rafter* — *Crown plate*

Construction of the roof trusses begins with the tie beams and the diagonal principal rafters. These rise from the wall posts at the divisions between each bay. The crown plate is also added now, and probably lifted into place with pulleys.

Building a building

A FINISHED BUILDING, ready for its occupants to move into, does not just appear overnight. Buildings are large structures that are costly and labor-intensive to put up, and a great deal of planning and work is involved in their construction. Work begins with extensive plans of the structure. The site then has to be prepared and leveled. Next, the main elements of the structure, which today include plumbing and electricity, are built. Finally, the building is decorated. This medieval-style timber-framed house shows the stages of a building under construction. The timbers are first cut to size. They are then added one by one, and the house is built up in a series of units called bays. Another method is to assemble part of the frame flat on the ground, and then raise it into place.

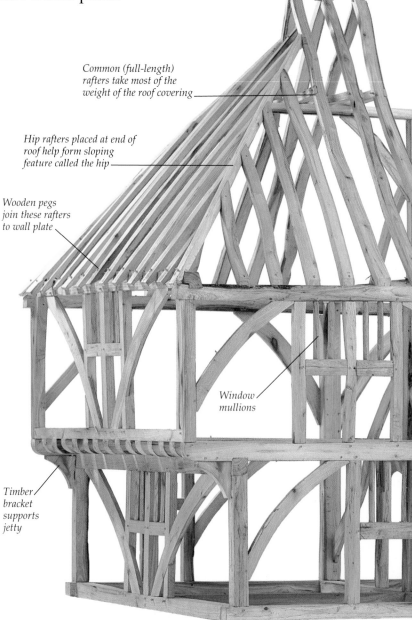

Common (full-length) rafters take most of the weight of the roof covering

Hip rafters placed at end of roof help form sloping feature called the hip

Wooden pegs join these rafters to wall plate

Window mullions

Timber bracket supports jetty

WATTLE AND DAUB

This was a common infill in the Middle Ages. Wattles, thin pieces of oak or hazelwood, are woven in and out of upright oak staves. This basketwork pattern is then fitted betwęen the studs of the timber frame. The daub, a mixture of clay, dung, and chopped straw, is applied on either side. This may then be covered with a smoother plaster before being painted.

Oak stave | *Wattle* | *Daub* | *Plaster*

PUTTING IT TOGETHER

These 16th-century carpenters are assembling a timber-framed house. While a group of men use a rope and pulley to raise one of the heavy beams, two others cut timber. A third, perched on the wall plate, uses a hammer to secure a principal rafter.

6 CROWN POSTS AND COMMON RAFTERS

The roof trusses are completed with the large branching crown posts. On this building they are plain. Often, however, these posts were left exposed and were carved to resemble stone pillars with capitals. Meanwhile, the common rafters are added between the principal rafters. The overall shape of the building emerges: a house of four bays, the middle two forming a two-story hall.

7 THE COMPLETE BUILDING (above)

The spaces between the studs are filled with wattle and daub and the hipped roof is covered with tiles. When the building has been weatherproofed, work on the interior can be completed, and the outside decorated. Then the wattle-and-daub panels are painted white and the timbers a red ocher color that was widely popular in Europe during the Middle Ages.

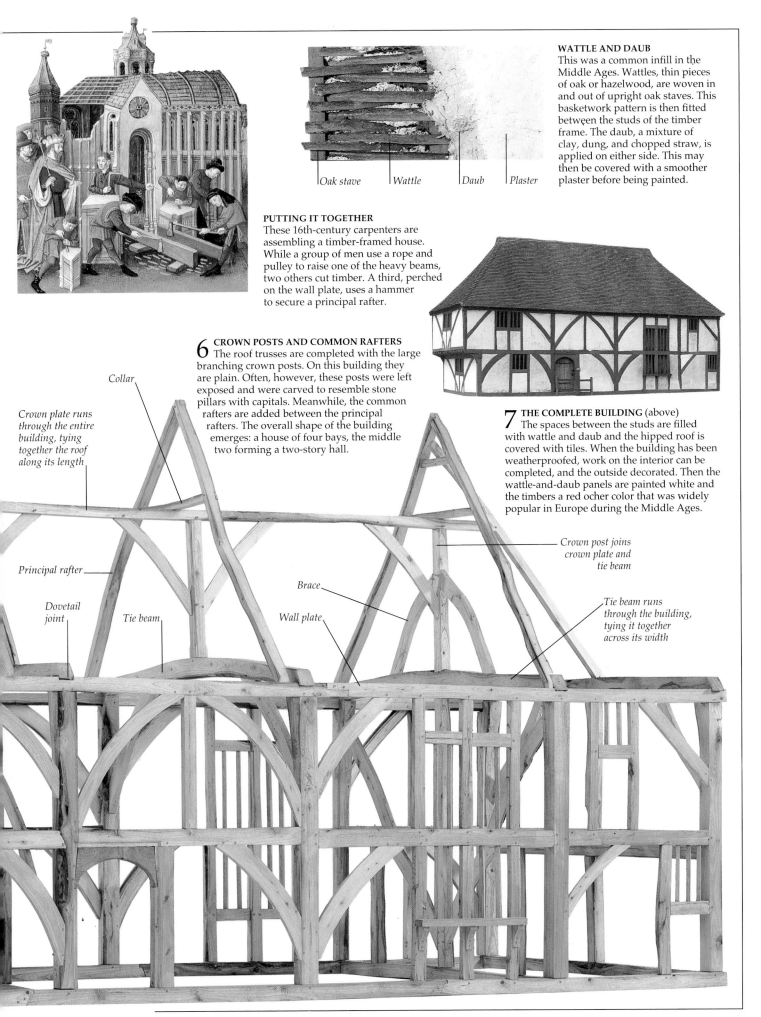

Collar

Crown plate runs through the entire building, tying together the roof along its length

Principal rafter

Dovetail joint

Tie beam

Brace

Wall plate

Crown post joins crown plate and tie beam

Tie beam runs through the building, tying it together across its width

Timber-framed buildings

TIMBER FRAMING, in which wood planks and beams form the structural elements, is one of the oldest methods of building. Timber-framed houses were built by skilled carpenters, who learned their craft during long apprenticeships. In a traditional medieval timber-framed building, the gaps between the timbers are filled in with bricks or with wattle and daub to form the walls. The upper timbers are covered with tiles or thatch to make the roof. In some areas, the owner's wealth was indicated by the distance between the timbers – the closer they are together, the more the house cost to build.

STORING THE GRAIN
Some of the biggest timber-framed buildings were granaries. This one from northern Germany was built in 1561. It has a wooden frame with diagonal braces at the corners. The frame is filled with panels of wattle and daub. An outside staircase, called a catslide stair, snakes up one side of the building.

COLOR COORDINATION
In the Middle Ages (c.1000–1400), oak timbers were often left unpainted, so that they weathered to an attractive silvery gray. Today, the wood is often painted black and the infill white, as on this house on the island of Funen in Denmark. Alternatively, people use a red ocher color for the wood and a creamy yellow for the infill. This is a common color scheme in France, Germany, and Scandinavia.

Bricks are laid in a herringbone pattern

WALLS OF WEALTH
Medieval magnates displayed their wealth by building houses with patterned timbers such as these (above). Diamond shapes are common all over Europe, while the four-sided or quadrant design was much sought after in parts of England.

STUCK IN THE CELL
For centuries, the market-place was the heart of many European towns. Often there was a timber-framed market hall. This one includes an open space for trading, a council chamber above – and a small barred room which was used as a prison.

UNDER ONE ROOF
This large German farmhouse (right) is of a type common in northern Germany during the 16th and 17th centuries. It is called an aisled house. Inside the double doors is a large threshing floor flanked by side aisles containing stalls for horses and cows. Living rooms for the owners and servants are at the far end.

Half-door provides ventilation for animal stalls

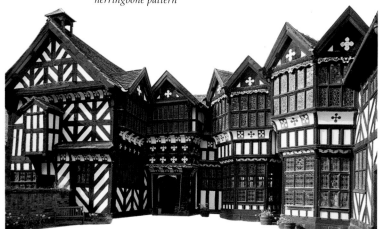

HALL OF FAME
Some timber-framed buildings were lavish affairs, for example, Little Moreton Hall, in northwest England. The large windows are a feature of English Renaissance houses, while striking patterns made by the wooden framework are typical of the grand timber-framed buildings of this part of England.

Wooden
shuttering
protects vent

Carving of hounds
chasing a hare

Wattle-and-
daub infill

Tall timber-framed townhouses
still dominate the old quarters of
many European cities. This fine
medieval house in the town of
Châteaudun, France, is known
as both the Porter's Lodge and
the Virgin's House. Several
patterns in the wood frame can
be seen, while stone or wattle
(thin wooden strips) and daub
(mud or clay) are used as infills
on different parts of the house.

STATUS SYMBOLS
To gain extra space in crowded
towns, medieval builders often
built out the upper floors
of a house to hang over
the street below. This
was called a jetty.
Because it was so
costly, a jetty was a
great status symbol
among the wealthy.

Jetty

Carved half-
rosette

Bust, possibly of
the original owner

An inscription records
the owner, Jost
Valpage, and the date
of the building, 1577

Valpage coat of
arms, added in
the 20th century

23

Supporting the roof

THE MOST COMMON way of supporting the roof of a building is with a wooden framework. In modern houses, this frame is usually hidden by the ceilings of the rooms of the top story. However, in older buildings, such as great halls and barns, the builders often left the timbers of the roof exposed. Over the years, carpenters have devised many different ways of putting roof timbers together. The roof covering itself is attached to timbers called rafters, but these are not usually sufficiently strong to support a wide enough roof. The roof either sags or the strain of the weight above pushes the side walls of the building apart. To compensate for this, various systems of diagonal braces and horizontal beams have been devised to hold the structure together and create a strong roof.

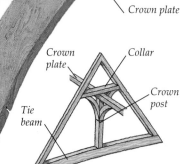

Wooden peg holds joints together

Collar

Crown plate

Brace

Crown post

Crown plate

Collar

Crown post

Tie beam

CROWN-POST ROOF
A popular early design was the crown-post roof. The crown post supports a beam called the crown plate, which runs the whole length of the roof. The crown plate in turn supports the collars, shorter beams running across the roof.

STRONG SUPPORT
This crown post has four concave braces, joining it firmly to both the crown plate and the collar. Each timber was attached with mortise-and-tenon joints (see p. 9), secured with wooden pins.

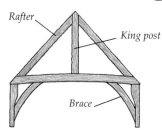

Crown plate

Brace

Tenon

BRACING WORK
Curved and diagonal beams, often called braces, are very important in roof structures. If two beams are joined at right angles they do not form a strong unit. The addition of a diagonal brace solves this problem. Braces can also enhance the appearance of a roof, and some, like this medieval one, were painted in bright colors.

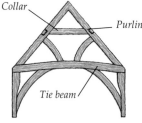

Rafter

King post

Collar

Purlin

Arch brace

Brace

Tie beam

Corbel

KING POST ROOF
This is one of the simplest roof structures, and was used often in the early Middle Ages. A heavy load passes down the king post to the tie beam, which usually sags. So braces were often added to help support the tie beam on either side.

COLLAR PURLIN ROOF
In this type, long beams called purlins run the length of the roof, tying the rafters together. Both a collar and a tie beam are placed across the width of the building, and various braces may be added to give extra strength.

ARCH-BRACED ROOF
In this design, pairs of curved timbers replace the tie beam. These timbers are supported on stones called corbels, which project from the side wall. This has the advantage that a wide span is covered and the roof space is left clear of timbers.

FOREST OF TIMBERS
The great market halls and barns of France and England often have magnificent timber roof structures that have never been concealed by ceilings. This market hall, at Martel in the Dordogne region of France, has groups of braces that radiate out from the crown plate like the spokes of a wooden wheel. This arrangement allows a wide span to be supported without the need for columns in the middle of the hall.

Main rafter

Subsidiary rafter

Hammer beams

Collar

Arch brace pushes against main rafters to stop them sagging

Brace supports hammer beam

Purlin runs entire length of roof, tying together main rafters

Carved angel

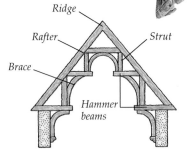

Ridge

Rafter

Strut

Brace

Hammer beams

HAMMER-BEAM ROOF
This is an ingenious design which probably originated in France. Timbers called hammer beams stick out from the sides, supported by curved braces beneath. As with the arch-braced roof, the hammer-beam is an open design, allowing one to see right up to the ridge of the roof.

CHOIR OF ANGELS
Hammer-beam roofs were used in the 15th century. Hammer beams, which are beautiful but very complicated, were used only on important buildings such as the great halls of large houses and big churches. Sometimes, there is only one pair of hammer beams on each main rafter. But on buildings of the highest status, like this church at Woolpit, England, there are two, making what is called a double hammer-beam roof. To make the importance of the building even more obvious, the projecting ends of the hammer beams were often adorned with carvings – angels were a popular subject for the builders of eastern England.

Covering up

TRADITIONAL ROOF COVERINGS varied from place to place, depending on what was available locally. Thatch (see pp. 30-31) was widely used, but stone tiles or slates were also popular in areas where the raw materials could be readily found. Wooden shingles, usually made from oak, were an option where there was a good supply of lumber. However, in places where people had learned to fire clay to make bricks, roofs were more often covered in clay tiles. The ancient Greeks and Romans roofed their temples and villas with tiles; these are still common in Mediterranean countries. Tiles have two big advantages over thatch – they are fireproof and they are very long-lasting. In addition, they can be made in different sizes and shapes, with curved edges for a fish-scale effect, or with pointed ends for a diamond pattern.

ROOFTOPS
Bright red tiles cover most of the roofs at Roquebrune in the south of France. Curved tiles, as seen on many of the roofs here, have been used since the time of the ancient Greeks. They are called pantiles and are also commonly found in places as far apart as Holland and California.

Clay tile

Slate

Sandstone tile

A MULTITUDE OF MATERIALS
Clay is a material that is easily shaped and molded, and clay tiles come in all shapes and sizes. Most are made to a standard size, and they are very popular. Slate is not as easy to mold, but the tiles are thin and lightweight, so they do not require heavy support structures. Stone tiles, on the other hand, make a heavy but very durable roof surface. They are generally used only where this material is plentiful.

FISH SCALES
In some areas it was traditional to cover outside walls with tiles, often in a decorative fish-scale pattern. In the 19th century, roofers began to imitate these walls, using both slates and tiles with pointed and rounded ends (right). Often this treatment was kept for a feature, such as the roof over a bay window.

FIXED IN PLACE
A view of the underside of a tiled roof shows the thin horizontal wood strips, called laths, nailed to the larger rafters. Each tile is securely attached to the laths with wooden pegs and overlaps its neighbors above and below.

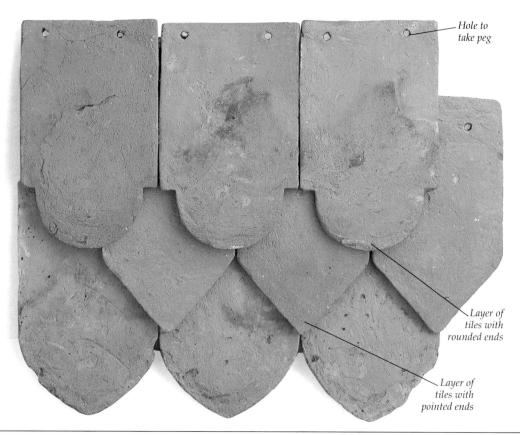

Hole to take peg

Layer of tiles with rounded ends

Layer of tiles with pointed ends

Grotesque mythical animal
made from glazed ceramic

PARADE OF THE GROTESQUES

In traditional Chinese architecture, the roof is one of the most important elements in the whole building. Sometimes the roof is designed even before the rest of the structure. On the grand entrance halls of the Imperial Palace in Beijing, the roofs are elaborate structures covered with yellow tiles. Only the emperor could use this color on his roofs. This is the roof of the Hall of Middle Harmony.

Endpiece roof tile

Etruscan terracotta antefix of the 6th century B.C.

Ceramic endpiece roof tile of the Ming dynasty

ENDPIECE

This yellow tile was one of many that decorated one end of the roof of an imperial Chinese building of the Ming Dynasty (14th to 17th centuries).

EDGING THE ROOF

On some ancient buildings, decorative tiles called antefixae were attached along the lower edge of the roof to hide the ends of the tiles. This terracotta antefix comes from an Etruscan building in Capua, Italy.

REGIONAL ROOF PATTERNS

In some areas, roofs display colors and patterns typical to the region. One of the more striking examples is the fashion for multicolored tiles arranged in geometrical patterns in Burgundy in France. The color of slates, another popular roofing material, varies enormously – from dark olive green to light blue, purple, red, or gray. However, other effects can be achieved with more muted colors. In some parts of the U.S., gray wooden tiles or shingles cover the roofs of farm buildings, many elegantly patterned in rectangles.

Yellow and black tiles, Beaune, in Burgundy, France

Wooden shingles, Nevada

Gray, curving slates, Eltville, Germany

On the roof

I$_N$ DRY CLIMATES, roofs are often flat. But in most countries they are sloped so rainwater or melted snow drains off. The water streams into a metal or wooden gutter and down pipes to the drains below. In many places, especially where the walls are made of vulnerable materials such as earth, builders allow a generous overhang on the roof which would keep the walls from getting wet. Pitched, or sloping, roofs can take many forms. Windows for attic rooms can be installed in gables, in the upright portion of a mansard roof, or as dormers that stick out from the slope of the roof. Roofs are often decorated with much ornamentation, since they are high for all to see.

ROYAL RESIDENCE
A chief on the Trobriand Islands in the western Pacific traditionally lives in a house with tall gables. The thatched gables are highly ornate, indicating that an important person lives in the house. The decoration consists of painted reeds and cowrie shells. These shells are especially valued in Trobriand culture.

DORMER WINDOWS
Windows like this stick out from the main line of the roof and are topped with little roofs of their own. Sometimes dormer windows show where the roof area has been converted to provide more living space. Often they are built in from the start to save money on the stone or bricks needed to build the walls higher. They also make a picturesque roof line.

TALL AND GRACEFUL
Many of the larger town houses in the north of Germany have tall, ornate gables like these on two fine merchants' houses in the market place of Lemgo. They are decorated with semicircular scalloped designs and topped with stone finials. These features make the houses stand out above their neighbors. The builders managed to cram as much as four storys of extra accommodation into these tall, graceful roofs.

Stone finial

Coat of arms

Scalloped decoration

Sundial

Small, flat-roofed extension to main building

ALL IN A ROW
From the 16th century, Amsterdam expanded as a port and financial center. Rich merchants built fine houses there with elaborate gables – some triangular, some curved, and others with a stepped effect.

Decorative gables

A gable is the triangular part of a building between the top of the side walls and the slope of the roof. In some buildings, the gables are hidden away at the ends of the structure and are hardly visible at all from the front. But in many places, architects have realized that gables have great potential. They can have windows built in, throwing light into otherwise dark rooms in a roof space. They also provide a superb opportunity for display – they are the tallest part of a building's walls, they lend themselves to all sorts of decorative effects from stone carving to painting, and they can transform a building from something plain and ordinary into an outstanding landmark.

HIPPED ROOF
The sloping ends show that this Danish house has a hipped roof – a roof in which there is no gable. Instead, there are four sloping faces, including triangular ones at either end which slope up and in toward the ridge. A hipped roof saves on walling materials, which may be an advantage where stone is scarce. But it leaves less space for storage.

MANSARD ROOF
Named after the 17th-century French architect, Jules Hardouin Mansart, this roof has sides with a steep lower slope and an upper section that is flatter. The almost vertical lower slope allows the builder to include large rooms in the roof.

Gilded ornament at apex

Edging tiles

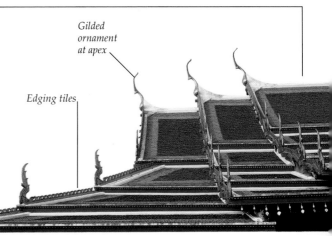

HANGING OVER THE EAVES
Roofs on temples and important buildings in the Far East usually have a generous overhang at the eaves. This feature probably began as a way of throwing off the rain, but it developed into a way of making the roof more showy – roofs often have an upturned profile, different colored tiles, and there are frequently sculptures of dragons and other mythical beasts lining the ridge.

PUEBLO HOUSES
In dry and desert areas, traditional mud-brick houses often have flat roofs. Any rain that falls can be drained off through spouts that stick out of the sides of the houses. Wooden ladders give easy access to the roof, which provides a spacious working or living area when the sun is not too hot.

Carved infill panel

A RIOT OF CARVING
A gable facing a town street is an ideal place for a special display of craftsmanship and to show the status of the building's owner. These particular gables are on large middle-class German houses. The timbers of the framework are lavishly carved and painted, and extra wooden panels have been built for additional carvings.

Shuttered window

Wattle and daub infill panel

Scalloped motif

Carved beam

Tiled roof

Carved jetty

Thatching

PREPARING THE THATCH
Water reed is a popular material for thatched roofs. Once the reeds have been harvested and tied into bundles, they are ready to be used on the roof. Straw requires more preparation. It is dampened to make it more flexible, before being made into small bundles called yealms. The thatcher runs his fingers through the yealms to remove any short straws. Finally, six or seven yealms are put together to make a bundle for thatching.

T<small>HE FIRST HOUSES</small> ever built were probably covered with thatch. Through the ages, the materials used have varied from place to place and depend on what can be found locally. Straw or reeds are widely available and are still the traditional materials used for roofing in many parts of the world, from Africa to Europe. Sri Lankan houses are often thatched with palm fronds, and some buildings in the Hebrides, in Scotland, are covered with heather. Thatched roofs in northern areas of the world are often much thicker than those in the south, with the straw or reeds overlapped many times to keep out the weather. Some thatched roofs are beautifully decorated with traditional ornaments on, or ornate patterns near, the ridge.

MODEL VILLAGE
The village of Great Tew, England, was built by the local landowner in the 18th century. The houses were meant to provide comfortable accommodations for the workers on his estate. They are built of local limestone and roofed with reed thatch. In a design that is typical of the area, the roof plunges down below the level of the first-floor windows.

Ridge roll – a bundle of reeds laid horizontally

Feathers

Mallet, to knock in spars

Twister, to join wires together

Spar hook, to shave spars and rods

Dutchman

1 EAVE COURSE
The thatcher starts work at the eaves, or edge of the roof, and works up. The first material laid on the roof is the eave course. To straighten the thatch, the thatcher hits the yealms from below with a leggett. Then the reeds are fixed in place by long steel rods called sways. The sways are attached to the wooden rafters beneath with steel pins.

Steel sway holds reeds in place

THE LEGGETT
One of the most important tools for reed thatching is the leggett – a board with a long handle attached. The board is studded with nails or copper rings. The leggett is used to bang the ends of the reeds to straighten them.

Eave course – reed thatch laid at the eaves

TOOLS OF THE TRADE
Thatchers use a number of tools. Some of these are familiar because they are used in other trades. For example, the thatcher uses a mallet for knocking in the hooks that hold the thatch to the wooden timbers of the roof. Other tools are used only for thatching. A twister is used to join wires together. The spar hook is a specialized knife that is used to shave the hazelwood spars that secure the thatch at the ridge of the roof. First a leggett and then a dutchman are used for knocking reeds evenly into position. Thatchers may also use long metal needles to sew thatch to the rafters at various points along the roof.

TIED DOWN
Some of the compact whitewashed houses on the Isle of Man, off the coast of England, have thatched roofs. The local style, shown in this example, is to tie the thatch down with rope secured to pegs in the gable of the house.

NEW ENGLAND THATCH
When the first European settlers reached the east coast of North America in the 17th century, they took traditional English skills with them. They built wood-framed thatched houses like this one at Plimouth Plantation, Massachusetts.

2 BROW AND FULL COURSES
The thatcher now adds a brow course and two full courses. Each course is placed higher up the roof and overlaps the one beneath. This means that the metal sways of the lower courses are covered. Each course is secured with its own sway. At the ridge, or top, of the roof, long bundles called ridge rolls are laid horizontally.

Wrapover ridge thatch of sedge grass

Hazelwood spars secure thatch on ridge

3 COVERING THE RIDGE
A more flexible material is used for the thatch on the top of the roof, because it has to wrap over the ridge. On this roof, the thatcher has used straw and sedge grass. Both are laid over the ridge and secured with lengths of hazelwood called spars. Between the spars, cross-rods, also made of hazel, are arranged. Together the spars and cross-rods make up the ligger. When the wrapover ridge is fixed in place, the ends are trimmed with a sharp knife or spar hook.

Cross-rods used to decorate ridge

Ends trimmed with a sharp knife or spar hook

Straw

ROUND HOUSES
The traditional round houses of Africa are always roofed with thatch, as are these buildings from northern Nigeria. The usual method of thatching is to lay the straw with the heads of grass pointing downward, the opposite direction to that favored in Europe.

Second full course of reeds

Brow course

First full course of reeds

Columns and arches

WHEN EARLY BUILDERS wanted to bridge a gap created by a door, window, or other opening, they placed a straight wooden beam or stone block called a lintel across the top. But the bigger the gap, the thicker the lintel needed to be. Large, heavy stones are hard to lift. An arch, built of small stones or bricks and supported by columns, can span a wide opening and is a better solution. During building, the stones are supported by a wooden framework, called centering, until the keystone at the top of the arch is fitted. The ancient Egyptians and Greeks used arches, but the Romans were the first to build them on a large scale. Roman arches were semicircular; these were popular until Gothic masons invented the pointed arch in the Middle Ages. Today, strong lintels can be made with materials such as steel and concrete, so arches are less common than they once were.

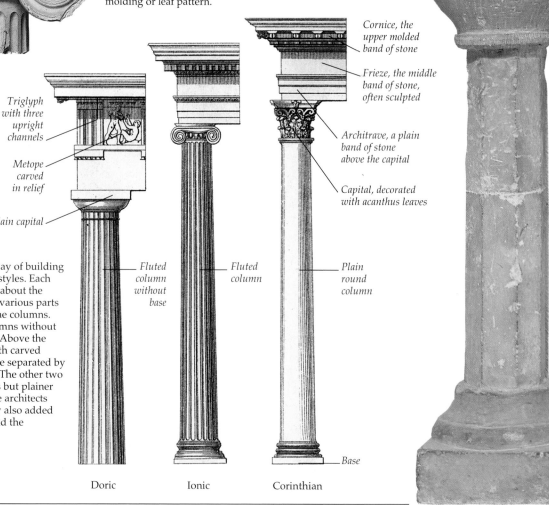

Spiral scroll or volute

Abacus, a narrow band of stone

GREEK IONIC CAPITALS
At the top of a column there is usually a capital, which connects it to the arch or lintel above. Greek Ionic capitals always have pairs of spiral scrolls, known as volutes. Between the volutes there is an area called the echinus, which is carved with "egg-and-dart" molding. Just above the volutes is a shallow abacus, often carved with a horizontal molding or leaf pattern.

Echinus, or decorated band, with egg-and-dart molding

Cornice, the upper molded band of stone

Frieze, the middle band of stone, often sculpted

Triglyph with three upright channels

Architrave, a plain band of stone above the capital

Metope carved in relief

Capital, decorated with acanthus leaves

Plain capital

ALL IN ORDER
The ancient Greeks devised a way of building according to three "orders," or styles. Each order consisted of a set of rules about the proportions and appearance of various parts of their buildings – especially the columns. The Doric order has fluted columns without bases and very simple capitals. Above the column is a frieze decorated with carved panels called metopes. These are separated by plainer panels called triglyphs. The other two orders had more ornate capitals but plainer friezes. Roman and Renaissance architects imitated the Greek orders. They also added two of their own, the Tuscan and the Composite (pp. 56-59).

Fluted column without base

Fluted column

Plain round column

Base

Doric   Ionic   Corinthian

Round Romanesque-style arch

Pointed Gothic-style arch

Coarse dog-tooth ornament carved with ax

Fine nailhead decoration carved with chisel

Abacus

THE AXMAN COMETH
This round arch at Canterbury Cathedral, England, was erected in about A.D. 1110, when the cathedral was being rebuilt after a fire. A monk called Gervase wrote a description of the work that was done at this time at Canterbury. Gervase says that arches like this were carved using an ax, hence their simple, geometric dog-tooth decoration.

ENTER THE CHISELER
When building work was begun again at Canterbury later in the 12th century, the pointed arch, typical of the Gothic style, was being introduced. Gervase reports that these later arches were carved with the aid of a chisel. This narrower, more delicate tool enabled the mason to produce much finer nailhead decoration.

Plain round column

Cushion capital

ARCHES ON STILTS
The Great Mosque in Córdoba, Spain, was begun in 785 by Apd ar-Rahman I, one of the Muslim rulers of Spain. He employed builders from Syria. To gain extra height they built the arches on stilts, using lower arches to give added strength. The striking striped appearance of the arches was achieved by using alternate pale stones and dark bricks.

Ogee arch

TWISTING AND TURNING
In the late Middle Ages masons experimented with new, highly ornate designs for columns. These extraordinary twisted columns at Ferrara cathedral, Italy, would not alone support the heavy load of the wall above. So the builders alternated them with the more usual straight columns, to strengthen the structure. The double-curved ogee arches, their points formed by two S-shaped curves, are also typical of the late Middle Ages.

Base

Vaults

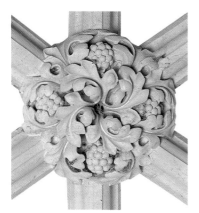

FOR MANY CENTURIES, the easiest and strongest way of creating a solid arched roof was to build a vault. Vaults are usually made of stone or brick, making them much heavier than timber roofs. The earliest styles, such as the Roman barrel vaults, were inadequate for coping with the structural stresses caused by their weight – their walls tended to inch outward. But with the introduction of groins, and later ribs, builders found a way of supporting the weight and making the whole structure stronger. Vaults can be beautiful as well as functional, giving an interior a grand, soaring appearance, and they are popular with designers of large churches and public buildings.

DECORATING THE BOSS
Where vaulting ribs met, masons fixed large stones called bosses. Bosses were often intricately carved, especially the largest one at the center of a roof. This 19th-century boss is decorated with fruit and foliage. Other popular subjects were faces and coats of arms.

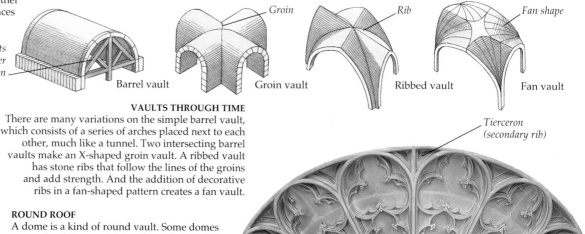

Centering supports vault under construction

Barrel vault

Groin

Groin vault

Rib

Ribbed vault

Fan shape

Fan vault

VAULTS THROUGH TIME
There are many variations on the simple barrel vault, which consists of a series of arches placed next to each other, much like a tunnel. Two intersecting barrel vaults make an X-shaped groin vault. A ribbed vault has stone ribs that follow the lines of the groins and add strength. And the addition of decorative ribs in a fan-shaped pattern creates a fan vault.

ROUND ROOF
A dome is a kind of round vault. Some domes are made of stone or brick, others of a lightweight material covered with sheet metal. The metal gives a weatherproof surface that glitters and shines in the sun. It was often used on religious buildings, such as the Dome of the Rock in Jerusalem.

Tierceron (secondary rib)

Carved stone ornamentation

Panel

Shaft

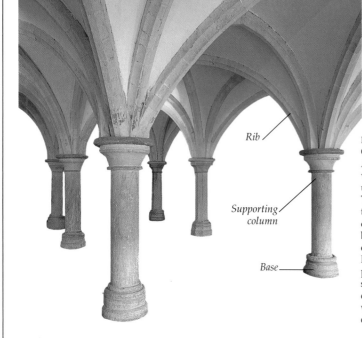

Rib

Supporting column

Base

FOREST OF RIBS
Gothic masons of the Middle Ages built some of the finest vaults, with ribs thrusting upward to form pointed arches. These arches made it easier to vault spaces of varying dimensions. This ribbed vault, built in 1202-24, is in the crypt of Rochester Cathedral, England. Vaults like this were popular for roofing the high spaces of large churches and cathedrals; they were also widely used in crypts and cellars in castles and churches.

FANNING OUT
English masons of the 16th century introduced the fan vault. It has ribs of equal length that spread out in a semicircle or quarter-circle to make a shape like an opened fan. These vaults are often better for decorating than for holding up heavy structures. They were often used to roof small side chapels in churches or cathedrals.

Large
central boss
with carved
foliage

Lierne
(small
cross-rib)

Main ridge
rib passes
along apex
of roof

Small boss with
stylized flower at
intersection of rib

Rib passes
across width
of roof

Pointed arch is
in the style of the
late Middle Ages

Plain capital

GOOD IMITATION
When 19th-century architects
began to revive the Gothic style
of the Middle Ages, they often
included vaults, in houses as
well as in churches and public
buildings. This vault is a type
of ribbed vault that has extra
small cross-ribs called liernes.
There are finely carved bosses
at the intersections of the ribs.
   The buildings of the 19th
century are sometimes quite
unlike the medieval structures
that inspired them, but this
19th-century design closely
followed the Gothic style.

Column
made up of
group of
small shafts

Base

Reach for the sky

TOWERS OF NOBILITY
The most powerful people in a medieval Italian town were the local nobles. Noble families built watchtowers as places of refuge in times of trouble, and, above all, as signs of status. The higher your tower, the more important you were. The town of San Gimignano in northern Italy still has 13 towers – originally, there were more than 70.

FOR THOUSANDS OF YEARS, people have been building towers for a variety of reasons. A tall tower can be an effective defense, enabling the occupants of medieval cities and castles to spot enemies – and shoot at them if necessary. A tower can also be a religious symbol. The pyramidal towers of Hindu temples represent the mythical Mount Meru at the center of the universe, and the spires of Gothic churches seem to reach toward the Christian heaven. In modern, crowded cities such as New York and Hong Kong, towering apartment buildings save on space by housing the maximum number of people in the smallest area.

Ornate spire tapers by stages toward an openwork top

This spire, although of Gothic design, has an unusual twisted effect

Lead provides flexible and long-lasting covering for spire

Broach support at base of spire

CALL TO PRAYER
Islamic mosques usually have at least one minaret – a tall, slim tower topped by a balcony. At set times each day, an official called a muezzin climbs the minaret to call the faithful to prayer. Minarets, like this one at Isfahan, Iran, are often decorated with colorful patterned tiles.

ONION DOMES
These strikingly patterned onion-shaped domes, built in the mid-16th century, top St. Basil's cathedral in Moscow, Russia. They are typical of the Orthodox churches of Russia and eastern Europe. These domes are raised on a tall, cylindrical structure called a drum, which gives them extra height and makes for a stunning skyline.

POINTING TO HEAVEN
The spires of the Gothic churches of the Middle Ages point to the sky, enticing the faithful to look up to the heavens. The spires of St. Nicholas's Church in Lemgo, Germany, built in the 1560s and 1660s, continue this tradition.

SKYSCRAPER SKYLINE
By the late 19th century, builders in the U.S. had mastered the art of making iron and steel frames for buildings. This, together with the development of safe passenger elevators in 1852, heralded the beginning of the age of skyscrapers. The first, the ten-story Chicago Home Insurance Building, was built in 1883. Many others were erected in American cities such as New York (above) and Dallas. They jostle for space high up in the clouds, and have transformed the modern city skyline forever.

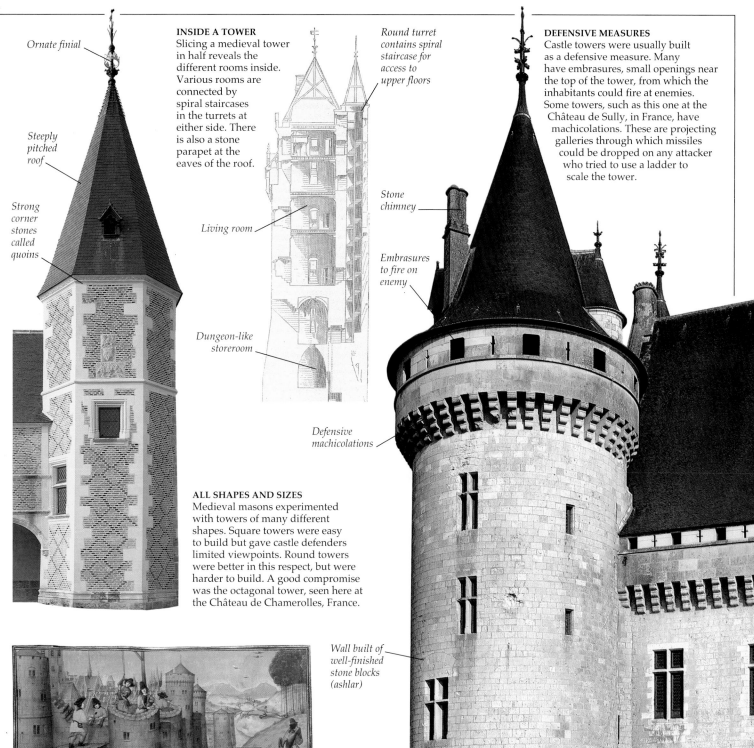

Ornate finial

Steeply pitched roof

Strong corner stones called quoins

INSIDE A TOWER
Slicing a medieval tower in half reveals the different rooms inside. Various rooms are connected by spiral staircases in the turrets at either side. There is also a stone parapet at the eaves of the roof.

Round turret contains spiral staircase for access to upper floors

Living room

Dungeon-like storeroom

DEFENSIVE MEASURES
Castle towers were usually built as a defensive measure. Many have embrasures, small openings near the top of the tower, from which the inhabitants could fire at enemies. Some towers, such as this one at the Château de Sully, in France, have machicolations. These are projecting galleries through which missiles could be dropped on any attacker who tried to use a ladder to scale the tower.

Stone chimney

Embrasures to fire on enemy

Defensive machicolations

ALL SHAPES AND SIZES
Medieval masons experimented with towers of many different shapes. Square towers were easy to build but gave castle defenders limited viewpoints. Round towers were better in this respect, but were harder to build. A good compromise was the octagonal tower, seen here at the Château de Chamerolles, France.

Wall built of well-finished stone blocks (ashlar)

Large windows probably added later – castles usually had small ones near the ground

TOWER BUILDERS
This medieval manuscript shows workers building town walls around Marseilles, France. Masons had little machinery but could usually call on plenty of laborers to help them. Here you can see workers carrying stone to the masons, using wooden hods and wheelbarrows. This material was often carried up a partially completed staircase in the tower. Another method was to use a simple hoist with a rope and pulley, which is shown rigged up inside the tower. The wooden platform shown on one wall gave builders access from the outside.

Staircases

Wrought-iron baluster, 1785

Cast-iron baluster, 1850

THE FIRST BUILDINGS were single-story, but in warm areas such as the Middle East, people used the flat roofs for extra living space. First, they made ladders to reach the roof. Later, they built simple stone or wooden steps. By the time of the Romans, who built the first apartment complexes, staircases were common. Many different forms evolved. Stone spiral staircases were popular in the Middle Ages, but straight wooden ones are most common today. After the Renaissance, the important rooms of large houses were usually on the upper floors, so outside entrance stairs often led up to the second floor.

Pointed finial

Baluster

Newel post

WROUGHT OR CAST
The balusters, the uprights supporting the handrail, can be the most ornate parts of a staircase. In the 18th and early 19th centuries, they were often individually made from curving lengths of wrought iron. Later 19th-century iron balusters, by contrast, were often mass-produced in a mixture of classical, Gothic, and baroque styles.

TURNING AND TURNING
Even a staircase built in a narrow stairwell can be an imposing sight, as shown by this 17th-century staircase. Like many others of the period, it is made of oak. The balusters have been turned by a machine called a lathe. The large corner posts, called newel posts, are deeply carved and have tall, tapering finials. Ornate balusters and newel posts were common in grander buildings after the Renaissance period.

Tread

Handrail

Baluster

ESCAPE ROUTE
On tall modern buildings, it is always important to have fire escapes. These staircases need to be on the outside of the building, with a landing on every floor for easy access. New York City offices and apartment buildings often have cast-iron fire escapes, like this one in the SoHo district.

Painted cast-iron baluster, 1840-1855

IRON SPIRAL
After the Industrial Revolution, iron was used extensively in building. The individual parts of a staircase would be cast separately and bolted together on site. Space-saving staircases were often made in this way.

ROYAL STAIRCASE
Some staircases are highly ornate. This ceremonial staircase in an octagonal tower was built in France, at the Château de Blois, by King François I in the 16th century. Members of his court could look over the sides to welcome the king when he arrived to take up residence. The staircase is adorned with stone carvings of salamanders and the letter F, both emblems of the king.

Rounded finial

Carved scroll design

POINT OF ENTRY

Many Italian Renaissance buildings have their main rooms on the first floor, which is not at ground level but raised slightly. The entrance hall is usually reached by way of an outside staircase built of stone. It often has carved balusters and other ornamental details.

WINDING STAIRS

Many medieval buildings had stone spiral staircases. Such stairs were simple to build into a circular turret and had the advantage over wooden ones of being fireproof. They were also easy to defend. Because of the turn of the stairs, an attacker trying to climb up would find it difficult to use his sword.

Underside of tread

Newel, or central pillar

TOWER OF BABEL

The medieval period was a great age for tower-building. Castles and manor houses needed defensive towers, and many churches had bell towers. Most of these towers had stairs on the inside, but this illustration from the 15th-century *Bedford Book of Hours* shows a different design. The artist gave the mythical Tower of Babel an outside staircase, winding around the four sides of the building.

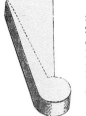

STEP BY STEP

Stone spiral staircases are made of pieces of stone shaped much like a keyhole. The pieces are placed one on top of the other, so that each makes up one tread and a section of the central pillar.

Stone tread

Fireplaces and chimneys

A ROARING LOG FIRE is a wonderful way of warming a house. Before chimneys and fireplaces, fires were built outside to avoid the risk of wood-and-straw houses going up in flames. But people soon found a way of keeping warm safely indoors. They built the fire on a stone hearth in the middle of the house, well away from the walls, and made a hole in the roof so that the smoke could escape. Gradually, masons began building stone fireplaces into the walls, and made chimneys that channeled the smoke safely up and out of the house. From the late 15th century onward, clusters of chimney stacks perching on the roofs of houses became a common sight, as fireplaces were built into almost every room.

COOK'S CORNER
This 18th-century German fireplace is full of useful features. A hood over the fireplace provided a spot for curing and storing meat, and a sunken hearth kept food warm. Salt and spices were kept dry in openings behind the small side doors.

HOME ON THE RANGE
This 19th-century range is another type of kitchen fireplace. A cast-iron unit combined several functions. It might contain one or two ovens, hot plates for cooking, shelves for warming pots, and an open fire to warm the room. A table provided an additional working surface.

Cobalt gives these tiles their brilliant blue color

Hood directs smoke up chimney

SULTAN'S SPLENDOR
The Palace of Topkapi in Istanbul contains elaborately tiled fireplaces. This one in the harem was designed by Sinan, the foremost Turkish architect of the 16th century.

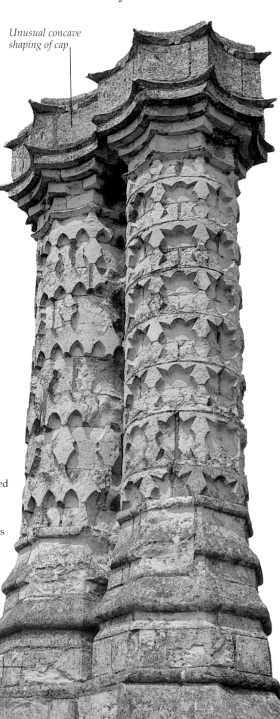

Unusual concave shaping of cap

STANDING PROUD
Tall chimney stacks grouped in pairs or larger numbers were something of a status symbol in 16th-century England. These stone stacks are from St. Osyth Priory. They are designed like miniature columns, with molded bases and caps like capitals. The richly carved central portions are even more decorative.

Molded stone base

HEARTH AND HOME
Source of warmth and comfort, the fireplace has become a symbol of home. This beautiful Renaissance fireplace in the Château de Sully in France draws on this idea. Above the fire, the mantel is decorated with a picture of another house, the Château de Rosny, commissioned because it was the birthplace of the 17th-century Duke of Sully.

LOTS OF POTS

In the days before central heating, large houses and apartment blocks often had a fireplace in every room. This meant that a large number of chimneys were needed. These chimneys often converge in a single unit on the roof, discharging their smoke from a series of earthenware pots. The curved covers on these pots prevent garbage – or confused birds – from falling into the chimneys. Pots were cheaper than stacks, and therefore popular in 19th-century Europe.

Crenelated caps

Details made of molded bricks

Special thin bricks form a corbel (bracket) for the cap

Molded necking between capital and column

Bricks are molded in a chevron pattern

POTS WITH A PURPOSE

These ceramic Portuguese chimney pots fulfill several purposes. A narrow opening at the top stops garbage from falling in. The pots are also designed so that wind does not whistle straight across a horizontal opening. Builders began making these pots during the 18th and 19th centuries.

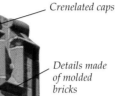

FIRE HAZARD

This North American log cabin has a stone fireplace and a wooden chimney. This traditional design gives protection where the fire is hottest. But there is also a risk of accidents when sparks fly up the chimney. Many house fires started like this before brick and stone chimneys were built.

CASTLES IN THE AIR

Some of the most magnificent chimney stacks crown Hampton Court Palace, England. The palace was built by Henry VIII's Lord Chancellor, Cardinal Thomas Wolsey. The chimneys are crenelated like tiny castle turrets, indicating the owner's status. When Wolsey's fortunes waned, he was obliged to give the palace to the king in an attempt to find favor – and the chimneys became symbols of royal power.

Wall and floor tiles

During the Renaissance, scenes from Greek and Roman mythology became popular decorative subjects. Stories were built up in a series of tiles, with each tile depicting a different character. The fashion continued in the 17th century, when the above tiles were installed around a fireplace at the Château de Sully, in France. They illustrate some of the exploits of Roman gods and goddesses, including Cupid (bottom left), the Roman god of love.

Sᴏᴍᴇ ᴛɪᴍᴇ ʙᴇᴛᴡᴇᴇɴ 3000 ʙ.ᴄ. and 2000 ʙ.ᴄ., a potter discovered that by giving his pots a hard coating, called a glaze, he could make them waterproof. He did this by covering the pottery with water mixed with powdered glass and a colored substance, such as cobalt or nickel. When the pot was fired, it became hard and non-porous. Around the same time, builders in the Middle East used tiles made of glazed pottery to cover mud-brick walls to keep them from crumbling in the rain. They realized that glazes could give the tiles beautiful colors, and used them to decorate walls and provide a hardwearing floor covering. Ever since that time, decorative tiles have been adorning the insides of buildings all over the world.

DELFTWARE
Tin-glazed earthenware such as this tile became popular in the Netherlands in the mid-17th century. Because it was manufactured mainly in the city of Delft, it became known as Delftware.

Fleur-de-lis

Diamond shape is called a lozenge

A GOTHIC PASSION
These tiles, with their fleurs-de-lis and rosettes in diamond panels, were designed by the 19th-century English architect A.W.N. Pugin, one of the foremost designers of the Gothic revival. The repeat pattern was manufactured at the Minton factory in England and fitted in a chapel in the 1830s.

Imperial minister

Attendant

IMPERIAL OFFICIALS
The Chinese had a highly sophisticated ceramics industry. Porcelain, a form of pottery usually made from China clay and a rock called petuntse, was invented in China during the Han Dynasty (206 B.C.–A.D. 220). It has to be fired at a very high temperature. By the 15th century, when this porcelain tile was made, detailed pictures in yellow, blue, and purple glazes were common. This tile shows three imperial ministers and their attendants.

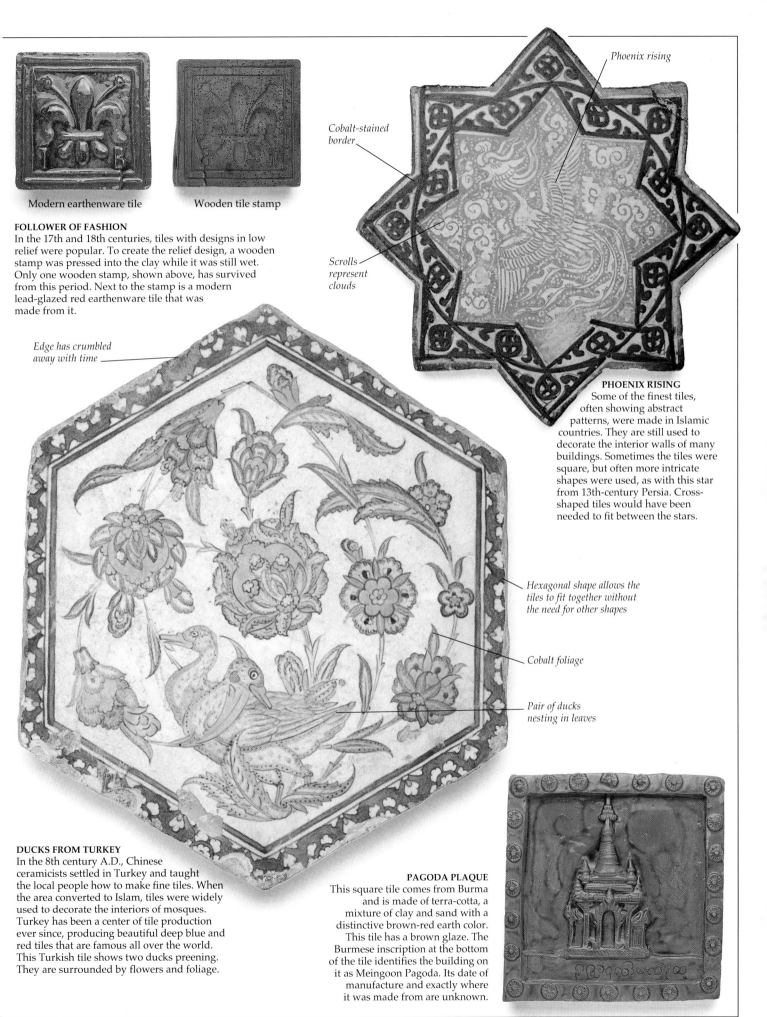

Modern earthenware tile

Wooden tile stamp

FOLLOWER OF FASHION
In the 17th and 18th centuries, tiles with designs in low relief were popular. To create the relief design, a wooden stamp was pressed into the clay while it was still wet. Only one wooden stamp, shown above, has survived from this period. Next to the stamp is a modern lead-glazed red earthenware tile that was made from it.

Phoenix rising

Cobalt-stained border

Scrolls represent clouds

Edge has crumbled away with time

PHOENIX RISING
Some of the finest tiles, often showing abstract patterns, were made in Islamic countries. They are still used to decorate the interior walls of many buildings. Sometimes the tiles were square, but often more intricate shapes were used, as with this star from 13th-century Persia. Cross-shaped tiles would have been needed to fit between the stars.

Hexagonal shape allows the tiles to fit together without the need for other shapes

Cobalt foliage

Pair of ducks nesting in leaves

DUCKS FROM TURKEY
In the 8th century A.D., Chinese ceramicists settled in Turkey and taught the local people how to make fine tiles. When the area converted to Islam, tiles were widely used to decorate the interiors of mosques. Turkey has been a center of tile production ever since, producing beautiful deep blue and red tiles that are famous all over the world. This Turkish tile shows two ducks preening. They are surrounded by flowers and foliage.

PAGODA PLAQUE
This square tile comes from Burma and is made of terra-cotta, a mixture of clay and sand with a distinctive brown-red earth color. This tile has a brown glaze. The Burmese inscription at the bottom of the tile identifies the building on it as Meingoon Pagoda. Its date of manufacture and exactly where it was made from are unknown.

Under your feet

THE SIMPLEST FLOOR is one made from the earth on which a building stands. The earth is sometimes mixed with lime or clay to bind it together, and then rammed down to make a flat surface. Until relatively recently, this was the most common type of floor in ordinary houses, and it is still widely used in developing countries. In time, people began to build floors with wooden boards supported by crossbeams called joists. More elaborate buildings had floors covered with stone flags, bricks, or tiles. Only in the grandest buildings – such as the villas of the Romans with their elaborate mosaic floors, or Italian Renaissance palaces paved with marble – was the floor a decorative feature. Today, most floors in the West are made of wood, and the popularity of carpets and other floor coverings means that the wood remains hidden.

MARBLE
Marble makes some of the most beautiful floors. It is valued for its different colors and textures as well as its smooth, cold surface. Marble can be cut accurately into small pieces using a saw, which enables it to be fitted into intricate patterns. It is also cool underfoot, making it popular in warm climates. This example comes from a house in Venice, Italy.

THE STYLE OF A TILE
Floor tiles, as well as being practical, can be decorated with colored glazes to produce a variety of patterns. These tiles (above) show two contrasting styles. Medieval circles and diamonds are surrounded by a border that is decorated with the swirling whiplash curves of the late 19th-century Art Nouveau style.

TILE BY TILE
Mosaics are pictures built up of small fragments of stone or colored glass, called tesserae. Because mosaics are tough, resistant to moisture, and do not fade, they became popular among the people of the warm and sunny Mediterranean. This section of a Roman mosaic floor comes from a villa at Halicarnassus in Turkey.

FISHY FLOOR
The ancient Cretans made mosaics out of pebbles, and by the 4th century B.C., the Greeks were putting mosaics together using tesserae. But the Romans were the greatest mosaic makers. They used several different methods, building up pictures with fragments of tile, pieces of marble, or stone and glass tesserae. These sea creatures are made from tesserae of stone and colored glass. They come from a 4th-century building in Carthage, Tunisia.

BURNING IN THE DESIGN

Many buildings in the Middle Ages had floors covered with encaustic tiles. This means that the design on these tiles was built up with inlays of different colored clays. These were then fired so that the design was "burned in." On this tile from the 13th-century chapter house at Westminster Abbey in London, intricate designs were created by inlaying a red earthenware tile with white clay. Two griffins crouch under a decorative frame, which was originally continued on three other tiles to make a large four-tile diamond.

Ornate border

Griffin

Red earthenware background

REPEATING PATTERNS

Popular motifs, such as the fleur-de-lis of France and the double rose of the Welsh Tudor dynasty, often decorated medieval tiles such as these.

Tudor rose

Fleur-de-lis

STONE

Stone is one of the most ancient and hardwearing of floor coverings. Because it is so heavy, it is usually only laid on the ground floor. By cutting stone into large flags, or smaller pieces such as these squares and hexagons, people can create a variety of interesting floor patterns.

SPIDER'S WEB

Oak, with its close grain, makes an attractive and durable wooden floor. This example has been laid in octagonal sections, making a pattern much like a spider's web.

Wooden floors

Wood is a very common flooring material. Boards laid on top of joists make a light, strong floor that can be used at any level of a building. The boards are often covered by carpets or rugs. They may also be laid in decorative patterns, or stained to bring out the pattern of the grain of the wood and left bare.

BEECH BOARDS

On this richly grained beech floor, pieces of beech have been varnished and bonded in strips. A thin band of neoprene (a type of rubber) separates and breaks up the color.

Doors and doorways

THE FIRST DOORWAYS were simply holes in a wall, covered by animal skins to keep out the weather. But people soon realized that a solid wooden door provided more protection. A door must be hung from a frame in the doorway. The top of the doorway may stick out slightly to form a dripstone, which channels rain away from the entrance. A doorstep is sometimes needed, since interior floor levels are often above ground level. Many doors are set back slightly, to give some shelter to anyone waiting to enter. But what makes doorways and doors different from one another is the way they are decorated. Decoration often gives important clues to where a door leads – for example, a church doorway may have carvings of saints.

An 18th-century dolphin door handle, England

A lion-head knocker from the 19th century, England

KNOBS AND KNOCKERS
Every door needs a handle, and some are finely designed in cast metal. In the late 18th century, metalworking was at its most ornate, and animal shapes like dolphins were popular. Doors can also have elaborate knockers in the shape of human or animal heads.

RECYCLING
In the Dark Ages after the fall of the Roman Empire, people often reused materials from abandoned Roman buildings. This Anglo-Saxon doorway in Colchester, England, was built with Roman bricks. The doorway has the typical triangular shape used widely in England before the Norman Conquest in 1066.

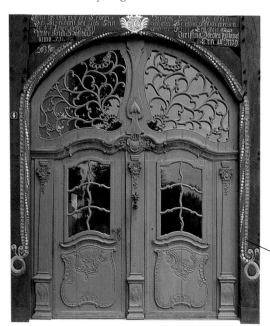

Richly carved and painted doorframe

LEAVING YOUR MARK
This German doorway has an inscription commemorating the merchant and his wife who first lived in the house. It was built for the couple in 1730, which is the date of the doorway. However, the door itself, designed in the swirling Rococo style of the end of the 18th century, was added in about 1790 by a descendant of the original owners.

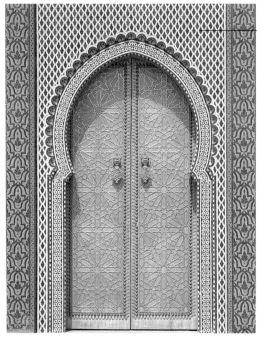

Shell-shaped decoration

GRAND ENTRANCES
Islamic buildings often have doorways with a horseshoe-shaped arch and shell-shaped decoration around the edge. The rich decoration of both door and doorway shows that this is an important building – it is in fact the Royal Palace at Fez in Morocco.

SIDE BY SIDE
The city of Dublin in Ireland grew rapidly in the 18th and 19th centuries, when many townhouses were built. They have elegant doorways, most with classical pillars and fanlights. The paneled doors are also typical of the period.

Semicircular fanlight

GOD AND THE DEVIL

Churches usually have a main doorway through which worshipers arrive. It is often designed to put people in the mood for a religious service. This doorway from a church at Kilpeck, England, was built in the 12th century. The carvings are a mixture of various Christian symbols and pagan animal forms.

Angel

Grotesque head, called a beakhead, with beak instead of mouth

Medallion with two fish, representing zodiac sign of Pisces

Zigzags typical of Romanesque doorways

Tympanum, or semicircular panel, showing grapes on the vine

Capital carved with lion

One serpent swallowing another, a symbol of Christ's descent into hell

Knight entangled in snakes

Mythical beasts symbolize people leaving the devil on the doorstep

Shaft richly carved with intertwining foliage

Carved sandstone figures

Windows

I<small>N ITS SIMPLEST FORM</small>, a window is a hole that lets in light and air while keeping out the heat or cold. Buildings have always had windows of some sort. Before the invention of glass, people simply kept out the weather with wooden shutters or animal skins. In order to protect themselves from the beating hot sun or the icy snow, many people built only very small windows. The shape and style of a window often provide clues about when it was built. Windows grew in size during the Middle Ages as glass became more widely available. By the Renaissance period, windows were often enormous and beautiful. The larger ones were surrounded by ornate details, like classical columns. Today, whole skyscrapers are sometimes faced entirely with glass.

ROUNDED OPENING
Window frames were not just functional but served an elaborately decorative purpose in their own right. This 12th-century round-headed window frame is carved with the heads of mythical beasts. Miniature columns, called shafts, support the arch of the window opening.

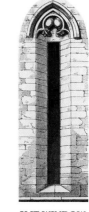

SLIT WINDOW
Because glass was expensive, early medieval windows were often just a simple slit in the wall. Sometimes the window had a flat top, sometimes a pointed head, called a lancet.

Dripstone

THREE IN A ROW
By about 1230, lancets were often arranged together in groups to form a window. Each lancet is called a "light," so this is a "three-light" window. Rain is diverted by the dripstone above.

SCREENING OUT THE SUN
In hot areas, particularly in India and the Middle East, a pierced screen called a *jali* is sometimes used in place of glass in traditional buildings. This screen lets in the fresh air and casts cool, dappled shadows inside the building. The wooden shutters can be closed at night and when the temperature is low. These jalis are in the town of Sanaa, in Yemen. Jalis are popular in Muslim countries, where their abstract patterns are an important way of decorating buildings.

Diamond-shaped pieces of glass, called quarrels, were common when glass was made in small pieces

Strips of lead, called cames, held the quarrels in place

Wrought-iron outer frame

Ornate wrought-iron catch

This glass is not the original glass – the window was reglazed in the 1930s

SHUTTING UP SHOP
Shutters are useful in hot countries. These shutters in Madrid, Spain, can be closed when the inner window is left open. Air circulates through vents in the shutters, but the hot sun is shut out, keeping the inside cool and airy.

OPEN-AND-SHUT CASE
A casement window can be swung open on a hinge, just like a door. This one was made in England in the 16th century. It has its own outer frame. This is unusual, since casement hinges were usually attached directly to the stone walls or the wood frame of the building.

EARLY TRACERY
By c.1250, the top of the window was often divided into a smaller circular area. Surrounding carved stonework, or tracery, also appeared during this time.

ELABORATE EFFECT
As tracery became more elaborate, shapes were arranged to make patterns in the head of the window. This example was built in 1277.

AT THE APOTHECARY
This fine bay (projection), finished in 1612, fronts an apothecary in the German town of Lemgo. The frieze illustrates ten of the most famous herbalists, doctors, and alchemists from the ancient world. Renaissance architects often included friezes or wall paintings of Greek or other mythical scenes in their work.

Finial

The steep gable is influenced by architects from the nearby Netherlands

Strap-work decoration

RIOT OF CARVING
During the 14th century, tracery became even more ornate. This window is smothered with ballflowers – ornamental balls surrounded by carved petals.

The tall, narrow windows are typical of northern Europe in the Renaissance period

A carved frieze of ten famous medics decorates the front of the building

This is one of several Ionic columns on the façade

Shallow, column-shaped pilasters decorate the façade

Ornamental finial

Pilaster

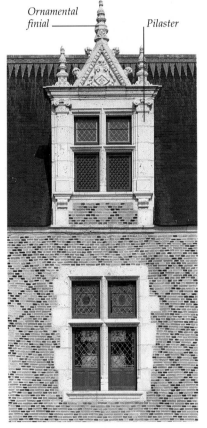

IMPRESSIVE ENTRANCE
The stone-framed windows of the Château de Chamerolles, France, stand out from the brick-built walls. Both of these two examples are typical of the French Renaissance style. On either side of the upper window are decorative pilasters in the shape of miniature classical columns. There is also a triangular pediment above this window, decorated with pointed ornaments called finials. All this informs visitors that they are looking at a building once owned by a person of great stature – in this case, the noble Lancelot Du Lac.

49

Stained glass

BLOWING GLASS
This 15th-century picture shows glassworkers taking gobs of hot molten glass and blowing into them to make bottles. Window glass was made in a similar way. A piece of molten glass was blown into a cylinder. The cylinder was then cut along one side while still warm, and uncurled to make a rectangle.

MONTH BY MONTH
This 15th-century stained-glass picture from an English country house is one of a series illustrating the months of the year. It shows a laborer harvesting crops.

DURING THE MIDDLE AGES, glassmakers found a way of using small pieces of glass to make a new kind of window. They realized that by mixing different chemicals (mainly metallic oxides) into hot melted glass, they could add color to it, or "stain" it. Small pieces of stained glass could then be arranged to make pictures. The glass was painted to add extra details, such as facial features or the markings on a flower petal. Stained glass has been used in ornamental windows ever since, in churches and public buildings as well as in large private houses.

Bull's-eye window

Steel-framed window, c. 1915

WOBBLY WINDOW
It is possible to make a glass pane by flattening one half of a blown glass globe. This creates a rounded shape, like the bull's-eye still seen in some windows (far left). Early methods of glass production meant that window glass was rarely flat or clear. The rippled effect of early glass is sometimes copied in more recent windows (left).

Green color obtained by mixing bioxide of copper with molten glass

Blue color made by mixing cobalt with molten glass

Red color made by mixing oxidized copper with molten glass

Window from Augsburg Cathedral showing the Old Testament prophet Hosea

ROSE WINDOW
Some of the best-preserved medieval glass, including this rose window, is in the cathedral in Chartres, France. There are some 22,000 sq ft (2,044 sq m) of glass in this cathedral, which was built in the early 13th century. Stained glass is often used in religious buildings. The rich blues and reds of the glass, and the fact that there is relatively little light-colored glass, make the windows typical of the period.

FRAGMENTS OF GLASS
During the 19th century, stained-glass artists were inspired by glassworking techniques of the Middle Ages. They used small fragments of glass to build up pictures, such as this strawberry flower.

OLDEST STAINED GLASS
These windows from Augsburg Cathedral in Germany were made in 1130, using methods that were to continue unchanged for centuries. The artist would begin by making a drawing on the white surface of a table. He then trimmed the fragments of glass to the right shapes and laid them on top of the drawing. Next, the colored pieces were painted with any extra details and fired in a furnace. Finally, the pieces were laid back on the table for leading.

Quarrel (piece of glass) is cut to match the exact shape of Daniel's hand

Bar separates two main sections of window

Lead came (strip) separates individual pieces of glass

Cames are soldered together at joints

Gaps between cames and glass are sealed with tallow (melted fat) to make them waterproof

Details of design are painted onto surface of glass

Window from Augsburg Cathedral showing the Old Testament prophet Daniel

Window from Augsburg Cathedral showing David, king of Israel

ABSTRACT PATTERNS
Modern glass artists often use the rich colors of stained glass to make striking abstract designs. This example is in Thula, in Yemen, where the strong sunlight throws colored patterns through the window and across the building.

SET IN STONE
People in the Middle East have been making pierced stone screens, or jalis (p. 48), for thousands of years. This man is using a similar technique to make a stained-glass window. He is cutting colored glass quarrels to put in position in the stone.

Finishing off

Leaf designs of
the 18th century
cast in plaster

WHEN THE STRUCTURE of a building is complete, and the windows and doors have been fitted, a number of decorative craftspeople take over. Plasterers smooth the walls, and often use their skills to decorate ceilings and cornices. In some places plaster is used on the outside of a house, to weatherproof mud walls or to create decorative effects. Then painters decorate the walls in different colors. If the building is an important one, they may even paint elaborate murals. Other skilled workers may decorate both the interior and the exterior of the building. Woodworkers often make decorative carvings, or fit paneling to the walls (p. 54). As the finishing touch, door fixtures and ornamental brackets, the products of metalworkers, are set in place.

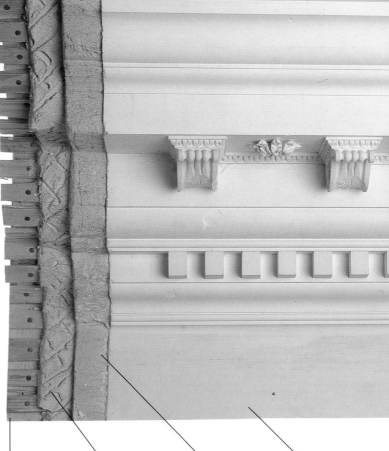

Wooden laths nailed to timber

Layer of coarse lime plaster under plaster of Paris, scored to help next layer stick

Second layer of plaster of Paris, shaped while wet with a rough template

Third layer of plaster of Paris, finely shaped with sharp-edged metal template

Boxwood mold

Composition molding

COMPOSITION
Made from a mixture of ingredients, including resin and linseed oil, composition, or 'compo,' was a popular plaster substitute in many 18th-century interiors. The material was mixed warm in a container that was standing in hot water. While still warm, it was pressed into ornamental molds. When set, composition was tougher than plaster, and useful for features such as fireplace settings. It could also be produced in a leathery state to fit around curves.

LOOKING UP
Plaster is an ideal material for molded ceilings. Intricate abstract designs, as well as animals and human forms, can be molded in plaster, as can be seen on this late 18th-century ceiling.

18th-century
wooden mold

The compo
molding for
a fireplace

Plaster

Most plaster is made of lime (made by burning limestone) and sand. Extra ingredients are added to give it strength. In the past, cow hair or dung was mixed in. Today, cement is used. A finer form of plaster is plaster of Paris, which is based on gypsum rather than lime.

Finished plaster ornament cast from a mould

Toothlike decorations called dentils in the style of an ancient Greek cornice

DAZZLING DETAILS

The roofs of Far Eastern temples are often a riot of bright colors. At the Pulguksa temple in Kyongju, South Korea, the timbers and dragon carvings have been detailed in a glorious mixture of blues, reds, and greens.

RENAISSANCE PANEL

The 16th century was a great age of painted interiors. This is a panel from a painted plaster ceiling in Kalmar Castle, Sweden.

Paint

In many early buildings, color was added to exteriors, or to interior walls to help brighten dark rooms. Limewash (one recipe for which was a mixture of soil, lime, sand, manure, and chopped straw) was often used on medieval houses. In grander buildings, the walls were sometimes decorated with painted murals. The Romans painted the walls of their houses in this way, and medieval churches were full of murals. Many were frescoes, where artists applied the color to wet plaster, which was then left to dry to a hard, permanent finish.

PLASTERING A CORNICE

Ornate plaster cornices like the one above, from an 18th-century house, were built in stages. First, the plasterer nailed wooden laths to the wall. Next he applied a coat of coarse plaster, made from lime and containing animal hair to bind the mixture together. Then he put on two layers of the finer plaster of Paris, gradually building up the detail.

FLOWERS AND FOLIAGE

Sometimes the normally white panels of timber-framed houses were decorated with murals. On the right is a 16th-century painted panel from a room in such a house. The entire room was originally painted like this, with even the timbers detailed in similar designs. Although not very colorful, the mural shows a strong use of line, much like the woodcuts of the time.

Continued on next page

Carved leaf and scrollwork

TREAD WITH CARE
A staircase is made up of several treads (horizontal boards) and risers (vertical timbers). When looking at a tread from sideways, it is possible to see the triangle that forms on the side of each tread. These triangles can be ornamented by the woodcarver, and they lend themselves well to scrollwork and foliage, as on this example from an 18th-century house. When this type of carving went out of fashion, the ends were sometimes boxed in with plainer wooden paneling.

Woodcarving

Woodcarvers provide some of the most spectacular ways of finishing a building. Carving on buildings is rare today, because the craft is highly skilled and labor-intensive – and thus expensive. But from the Middle Ages to the 19th century, carvings provided a fashionable way of adding a finishing touch to many buildings. A woodcarver might be employed to provide ornate fittings for rooms; alternatively, existing features, such as structural beams, could be carved when in place. The most popular places for carvings were inside, especially around prominent features such as doors and fireplaces. Sometimes an entire room would be fitted with carved wood paneling.

SEA MONSTER
A fireplace often forms the centerpiece of a room, so the wall above it and the fireplace itself are usually highly decorated. Instead of the usual plainer wood paneling that is often found in 16th-century interiors, the panels above the fireplace might be ornately carved. Popular subjects included coats of arms, family mottoes, the figures of Greek or Roman gods and goddesses, or bizarre mythical beasts such as this scaly sea creature.

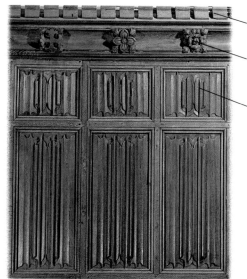

Dentil

Stylized flower

Linenfold panel

Corinthian acanthus leaf

DOOR DECORATION
Sometimes the door is the most important feature in a room. Doors and their frames are usually made of wood, so it made sense for the carpenter to pass them on to the carver for decoration. The jambs (the uprights of the doorframe) were often carved to imitate classical columns, or the top of the frame was ornamented with rich scrolls, as on this 18th-century example. The curling acanthus leaf shows the influence of ancient Greek architecture.

FOLD UPON FOLD
A popular way of finishing wooden paneling in the late 15th and 16th centuries was to carve it with a design called linenfold. This technique imitates cloth arranged in loose, overlapping, vertical folds. Linenfold paneling took much more time – and more timber – to make than plain paneling, and so was usually only found in the more important rooms of larger houses.

Side view

Front view

STANDING GUARD
Stokesay Castle is an English fortified manor house. It was begun in the Middle Ages, but additions were made in the 17th century. One corner of the later timber-framed wing is decorated with this carved wooden head, flanked by animals such as seahorses. With its long fernlike beard and leaves sprouting everywhere, the head looks like the gargoyles of the Middle Ages (pp. 60-61).

BRACKET (below)
Speculative building – when a developer builds houses for eventual sale – became popular in the early 18th century. Today, speculatively built houses are often constructed quickly, and much of the decoration is left to the future owners. But in the 18th century, speculative houses were as highly decorated as those built to order, with features such as this carved wooden bracket from a door case.

Molded beam

Corner post

LOOK, MA – NO JOINT!
Where a plastered wall meets a wooden doorframe, an unsightly gap can open up as the plaster shrinks while it dries. A wooden molding called an architrave covers up this gap when fitted around the doorframe, and improves the door's appearance. This design (right), with its circular roundels at the corners, became popular toward the end of the 18th century.

Gilt (gold-leaf) flower

Green man

BEAUTIFULLY SMALL
Sometimes a small decoration can be as effective as a mass of carving. This "green man" and the gilt flower above it are typical motifs in English design of the late 15th and 16th centuries. They decorate a wooden fireplace that was carved in 1485. The green man, his face interlaced with foliage, was a popular motif in medieval art. In fact, he dates back to the pre-Christian fertility gods of ancient Europe.

SKIRTING
Gaps often open up between the wall and the floor in a room. The area is usually covered by skirting boards. This piece of skirting was carved in the 1850s.

Wood stripped clean to show original carving

Paintwork was added later

A FINE FAÇADE
On very ornate houses, extra wooden panels, to take yet more carving, were sometimes added in areas which were usually filled by bricks or wattle and daub. These half-rosettes are carved on an additional panel on a house in the town of Lemgo, northern Germany.

Balconies

A BALCONY is a way of making the most of the open air without really being outdoors. Someone sitting on a balcony can have a good look at the view while still remaining close to the comforts of the interior. Balconies also work the other way around. In grand buildings they provide a place from which the inhabitants can be seen, while remaining at a higher level than the people looking at them from the outside – monarchs appear to their subjects and priests give blessings from balconies. Because they stand out from the front of buildings, balconies are usually given special architectural treatment. They are often ornately carved, or embellished with wrought-iron rails.

Scroll bracket

Brownstone masonry

HEAVE HO!
A wooden balcony and its supports are often made separately before being attached to the wall of a building. Once this balcony has been pushed into position and fixed, most of its weight will be carried by the wooden uprights.

CITY VIEW
This late 19th-century balcony in New York overlooks Riverside Park, one of the city's green spaces. Its stone platform is supported by a single heavy scroll bracket. It is decorated with classical acanthus leaves, which help the balcony stand proudly out from the front of the house. The balcony is not large, but it gives the residents enough space to stand and admire the view.

Acanthus leaf

Scroll bracket

IRONWORKER'S ART
The Art Nouveau architects of the early 20th century liked wrought iron because it could be bent into elegant curves that they often used in their designs. An ideal place to display this quality of wrought iron was on a balcony protruding from the front of a house, such as this one in Lima, Peru. The stone supports are also carved with typical Art Nouveau curves.

Swirling Art Nouveau foliage

Wrought-iron rail with whiplash curves

Painted wooden balusters

CUBAN CLASSIC
The round balusters that support the rail of this balcony in Havana, Cuba, recall the classical Renaissance buildings of Europe, as do the carved finials and mythical figures above. But the painted decoration, which catches the bright Central American sunlight, is much more typical of this part of the world. So, too, are the large open windows, which let in plenty of fresh air.

COLONIAL COLUMNS
The older houses in Sydney, Australia, sometimes have balconies on several stories. This provides plenty of space for sitting outside in the shade during hot weather. What makes these houses particularly distinctive is the ironwork – there are intricate rails, iron columns, iron arches supporting the upper levels, and iron balusters on the entrance stairs.

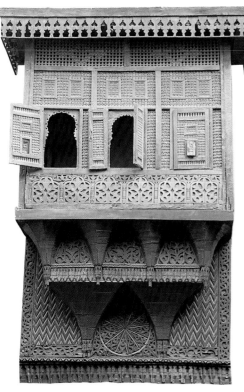

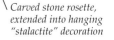

Overhanging canopy gives extra shade

Carved bracket helps to support canopy

Fluted column

CARVED IN WOOD
The wooden houses of Middle Eastern countries are often covered with intricate patterns, openwork screens, and false arches. A balcony or bay window, like this one in Cairo, Egypt, makes a perfect surface for this type of decoration, and an ideal centerpiece for a façade. The shutters and screens give shade – an important priority in hot climates.

CEREMONIAL PLATFORM
This is the balcony of a stone-built temple in Rajasthan, which, like many other Indian temples, is covered in carvings. Raised high above the surrounding ground, it has spectacular views across the desert sands. It provides a good stage for ceremonies, which can be viewed from the outside by a large number of people.

Carved stone rosette, extended into hanging "stalactite" decoration

Stone bracket

Carved bargeboard

THIS WAY IN
A porch like this one in Washington, D.C., offers shelter to people arriving at the front door. It also acts as a sort of signpost, telling visitors that this is the main entrance to the house. Finally, it provides a way of showing off some decoration – in this case, elegant wooden arches and carved bargeboards and supports.

Porches

In some places porches are quite small, covering just the area of ground in front of a doorway, and giving shelter to people entering and leaving the house. These small structures are sometimes called storm porches. But in other areas, porches are designed to be lived in, and can even extend all the way around a house. Many traditional American houses have large porches, which give shade in the warm months and shelter when it is cold. They have been used for everything from working to relaxing after a meal.

IN THE SOUTH
Vast two-story porches are seen in the southern states of the U.S. This porch in Georgia is given extra character by the circular tracery that fills the gaps between its wooden uprights.

UNDER COVER
Beneath the broad canopy of this porch in Hartford, Connecticut, there is plenty of space for a family to work or relax. One end is glazed for shelter from the wind, with panes of glass set in a pattern that echoes the woodwork.

Finishing touches

As WELL AS ADDING the finishing decorative touches, ornamentation provides a way of identifying building styles throughout history. In western architecture, fashions in ornamentation changed radically over the centuries, making it easy to guess the age of a building by looking at its decoration – ancient Greek palmettes, for example, are very different from the foliage used by Gothic builders in the Middle Ages. In China and Japan, however, ornamentation remained very similar for long periods, so it is more difficult for non-experts to date the buildings. There are many ways of decorating a building. Sometimes only the doors and windows are ornamented, but an important building, such as a large Islamic mosque, may be decorated all over.

EGYPTIAN LOTUS
The plants and flowers growing in and around the Nile River were a source of great inspiration for ancient Egyptian builders. These ceramic tiles are decorated with a lotus flower, one of the most common Egyptian decorative motifs.

Caricature of a king

GREEK MOTIFS
This beautiful ancient Greek marble fragment is crisply carved with a frieze of lotus flowers and palmettes – literally, "little palms." It comes from the temple of the Erechtheion on the Acropolis in Athens.

Stylized leaf

Ogee molding (made of combined convex and concave curves)

Abacus (flat stone at top of capital)

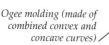

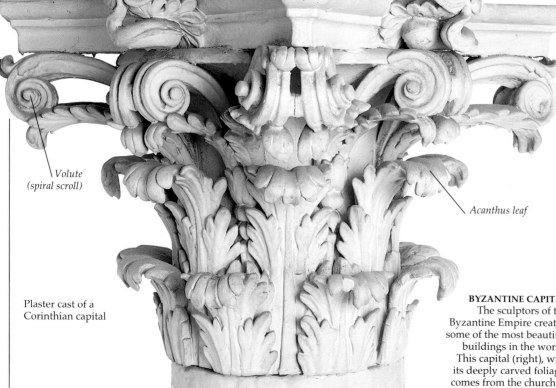

Volute (spiral scroll)

Plaster cast of a Corinthian capital

Acanthus leaf

A LEAF EVOLVES
The Romans adapted many of the decorative motifs of the ancient Greeks, including the three orders (pp. 32-33). The leaves on this Corinthian capital (left) are carved to look more like olive or parsley leaves, rather than the traditional Corinthian acanthus design.

BYZANTINE CAPITAL
The sculptors of the Byzantine Empire created some of the most beautiful buildings in the world. This capital (right), with its deeply carved foliage, comes from the church of Hagia Sophia, in Istanbul.

Devil with
batlike ears

Man with
flat cap

Monk
wearing a cowl

GALLERY OF GROTESQUES
In order to highlight the serenity of a Gothic church interior, grotesque carvings often adorned the outside of the building. Water spouts (a water spout carved in this way is called a gargoyle) and corbels (brackets) were carved with caricatures of local celebrities, or with images of the devil. The idea was that worshipers left this grotesque world outside when entering the consecrated space inside the church.

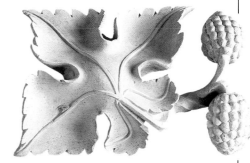

FRUIT FRIEZE
Gothic masons often carved foliage around arches and capitals. Early Gothic foliage was very stylized, while later carvings became more realistic. Sometimes the leaf was carved to fit into a rectangle or horizontal band, as with this raspberry leaf from a French chimney surround.

EARLY RENAISSANCE PANEL (above)
Renaissance artists experimented with a vast range of different ornamental styles. This carved stone panel includes beasts such as unicorns and monkeys, as well as stylized flowers in the roundels.

HEAD IN THE CLOUDS
The baroque ceilings of the 17th century were often painted to represent the artist's idea of heaven. This was usually a bright blue sky with fluffy clouds, populated by cheerful winged cherubs. A false perspective was often used, which had the effect of making the ceiling look like a real sky.

ZIGZAGS
The Romanesque style, based on rounded arches, groin vaults, and a modest use of moldings, became popular during the Middle Ages. These chevrons, or zigzags, were one of the most popular Romanesque ornaments. They decorated arches, doorways, and windows such as this one.

FLOWER POWER
Houses in the 20th-century Art Nouveau style are often decorated with sensuous curves and floral motifs. Majolica tiles – Italian ceramics glazed with bright metallic oxide – are often used to brighten the outside walls. This building in Vienna was designed by the architect Otto Wagner, who designed many elegant houses in the city.

59

Continued on next page

THE BEST IN INDIA
The best artists were recruited to make the marble inlays that decorate the walls of the Taj Mahal, in Agra, India.

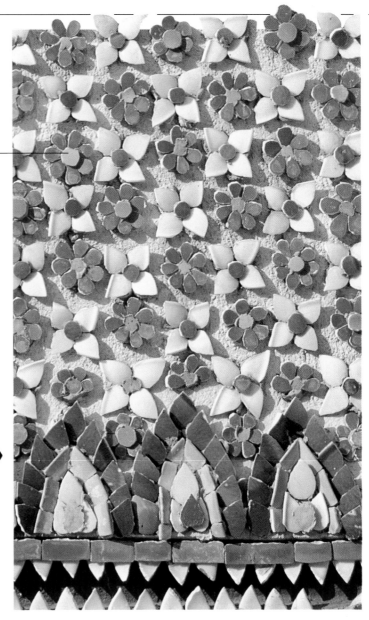

Flowers of colored porcelain

Eastern ornament

Countries such as India, China, and Thailand developed very distinctive styles of architecture, with their own typical ornamental motifs. In China, for example, the most common motifs are dragons (which were associated with the emperor), flowers such as chrysanthemums and peonies, and geometrical shapes such as octagons and circles. These decorations can appear in many different parts of a building, from roof tiles to silk wall hangings. Indian art has several different styles of decoration, from the intricate statues and friezes on the outsides of some Hindu temples, to inlaid marbles and precious stones in subtle, flowery patterns.

White marble provides background

Details in red agate

FLOWER PATTERNS (above)
Some of the Buddhist shrines of Bangkok are completely covered with decoration. As well as images of the Buddha himself, fragments of colored porcelain are used to make stunning floral patterns, which stand out in relief on the walls, as they do on this Thai temple.

HORSE ON THE ROOF
The roof of a Chinese building is often the most highly ornamental area. The hooves of this bearded warrior's horse are in fact resting on a roof tile. The pottery figure dates from the Ch'ing Dynasty (1644–1911). Its details are highlighted in rich green, yellow, and brown glazes.

FRUITS AND FLOWERS
Semiprecious stone inlays are often used as a way of embellishing the grander houses, temples, and palaces in India and Pakistan. This beautiful decorative inlay from northern India (left) features typical subjects – flowers and birds.

Multifoil arches make up the wall

These arches are blind arcading – they are purely ornamental

ORNATE ARCHES
The Alhambra, the palace of the Muslim rulers of Spain at Granada, is decorated with many typical Islamic designs – interlacing patterns, carvings that hang down from the ceiling like stalactites, and arches. Arches such as these (left), with multiple curves at the head of the structure, are called multifoil arches. They are common in Muslim buildings, especially in Spain and North Africa.

TURKISH TILES
These square earthenware wall tiles (left) form part of a wall panel. They were made in Iznik, Turkey, well known as a center for ceramic tile-making in the second half of the 16th century. Their flowing design and bright blue coloring are typical of tiles from Iznik.

Tomato-red color typical of late 16th-century Turkish tiles

Islamic ornament

Because the Islamic religion does not allow the realistic representation of people and objects in art, Muslim buildings are often decorated with abstract designs. Sometimes these designs resemble flowers and foliage, but the effect is usually very stylized. The most highly valued form of Islamic ornament is calligraphy, especially the writing of texts from the sacred book, the Koran. Ornament is usually applied to Islamic buildings with tiles, which lend themselves well to the kinds of repetitive patterns common in Islamic art. With their rich colors, and shapes ranging from squares to stars, Islamic tiles are among the most beautiful in the world.

WRITING ON THE WALL
This tile from a mosque of the early 14th century was stained with cobalt to give it a brilliant blue color. The inscription comes from the Islamic holy book, the Koran. It is written in a decorative script and detailed in low relief so that it stands out above the subtle background foliage. Tiles with inscriptions were traditionally placed at the height of the viewer's head, so that they were easy to read.

Building in difficult places

USUALLY BUILDERS CHOOSE a site that is easy to get to and simple to level and that will provide a firm foundation for a building. Sometimes, however, there are reasons to build in places that would otherwise be unsuitable – by a tall rock that is easy to defend, or by a marsh that is a good source of fish. The first inhabitants of Venice, Italy, for example, went there because it was hard to get to for the barbarians who had invaded Rome. Builders must use their ingenuity to invent structures that will stay standing in difficult conditions. Sometimes it is simply a question of having enough people to carry materials to an inaccessible site. At other times, an engineering solution is needed, such as wooden piles to make a building stand above water.

CITY ON THE WATER
Venice is built on islands in a lagoon. The buildings are supported on massive piles of pinewood that were sunk deep into the sand and clay beneath the water. Foundations of Istrian limestone resist corrosion from the seawater. The houses are connected by a network of narrow streets and by some 100 canals crossed by more than 400 bridges.

HANGING HOUSES
Houses were sometimes built on rocky outcrops for defensive purposes. After the Middle Ages, with the introduction of gunpowder and the change in the ways wars were fought, defense of individual buildings became less important. Houses were given larger windows, and even ornate wooden balconies like these at Cuenca in Spain.

Carved overhanging balconies

Stone defensive wall

HOUSES OF THE HILLS
In the inhospitable mountains and plateaus of central Turkey, wind erosion has left tall cones of rock sticking up where softer stone and soil have been blown away. Some of these structures have been quarried for building stone – timber is not plentiful in this area and many houses are built of stone. In the foreground, a number of these cones have been hollowed out to make houses.

AND IT ALL CAME TUMBLING DOWN
Certain parts of the world, such as the west coasts of North and South America, suffer from the effects of earthquakes. This frame house at Santa Rosa, California, was wrecked in the great earthquake of 1906. Modern steel-framed buildings can withstand quite powerful earthquakes, but they are costly to construct.

STILT HOUSES
In the tropics, houses on wooden pillars, like these in Port Moresby, New Guinea, are often built. These particular houses are modern in design but are built on traditional pillars, each made from an entire tree trunk. Houses built above water like this are useful on the coast, where they save valuable land and offer access to the sea for fishing.

WATER AT BAY
The ground on which this town in North Carolina is built is a series of islands connected by causeways. People are often attracted to marshlands because of fertile soil or because they earn a living from the sea. The ground on which the houses are constructed has been built up above the water level and is protected by retaining walls.

TO THE LIGHTHOUSE
Lighthouses are, by definition, usually built in difficult places, often on isolated rocks off the coast. The rocks themselves provide a good base on which to build, but it is often a difficult task to transport the materials through the sea to the site. And there is little or no space for the builders to work in when they do get there.

UP ON HIGH
People build on high, rocky outcrops for three main reasons. The earliest motivation was probably defense – you can see your enemies coming. Another was tradition – rocks are sometimes sacred places. The final reason, as in the case of the Summer Palace at Wadi Dahr, Yemen, is status – if you are a local leader, everyone can see how important you are.

Pierced screen shields interior from sun

Stone-built palace

Ornamental parapet provides superb vantage point

Tall outcrop of sandstone, produced by wind erosion

Index

Acknowledgments

Dorling Kindersley would like to thank:
Jonathan Buckley; Gavin Durrant; David Morgan; Martin Atcherley; Patrick Cooke and Mrs. I. Kempster of Athelhampton House, Dorchester; Dr. Simon Penn of Avoncroft Museum of Buildings; Jane Beamish and Alan Hills, British Museum; Charles Brooking and Peter Dalton, the Brooking Collection of Architectural Detail, University of Greenwich; Christopher Woodward of the Building of Bath Museum; Dr. Simon Penn of Avoncroft Museum of Buildings; Jane Beamish and Alan Hills, British Museum; Charles Brooking and Peter Dalton, the Brooking Collection of Architectural Detail, University of Greenwich; Christopher Woodward of the Building of Bath Museum; 52cl (private collection), 52-53t (Saint-Blaise Ltd); the Dean and Chapter of Canterbury Cathedral; Catherine Crook; Rudolphe Dupront, Château de Chamerolles, Chilleurs-aux-Boix, France; the Parish County Council and A. B. Manning, Kilpeck, Herefordshire; Christina Scull and Norman Grigg of the Sir John Soane's Museum; Mlle Debaque and Robert Bobet, Château de Sully, Sully-sur-Loire, France; Alastair West of the Thatching Advisory Service; Christopher Zeuner, Bob Powell, and Roger Champion of the Weald and Downland Open Air Museum, Sussex; H. D. Joosten of the Westfälisches Freilichtmuseum, Detmold, Germany; Ron Shipton of the Woodchester Mansion Trust. Helena Spiteri and

David Pickering for editorial help; Sharon Spencer, Susan St Louis, Ivan Finnegan, Kati Poynor, Aude van Ryn, and Sophy D'Angelo for design help; Giselle Harvey for additional picture research.
Models Thatch (30-31) made by Paul Lewis; Tudor Rose (18-19) carved by Jamie Vans
Illustrations by Richard Harris: 20l; Jason Lewis: 9br, 24-5; John Woodcock: 34m
Additional photography by Max Alexander: 6mr; Geoff Brightling: 13m, 16ml, 32-3, 34br; Peter Chadwick: 8-9; Peter Hayman: 12-13b, 58tl; Alan Hills: 27mr, 42-43, 60br; Mick Micholls: 58ml; Michael Moran: 56tl; Gary Ombler: 34tl, 35, 47, 48tl, 59bl; Harry Taylor: 16-17
Index by Hilary Bird

Picture credits
a=above, b=below, c=center, l=left, r=right, t=top

Adams Picture Library: 14cl, 36br, 40br; Ancient Art and Architecture: 16acl, 17acr, 38br / Chris Hellier: 58br; Arcaid / Lucinda Lambton / 1987: 22bl / Mark Fiennes: 30al / Roy Asser, 1991: 40cl; Archiv Fur Kunst Und Geschichte,

Berlin: 50br, 51bl, 51ar; Bibliothèque Nationale, Paris: 21al; The Bridgeman Art Library, London: 38ar / Bibliothèque Nationale, Paris: 19a / British Library: 9ar, 37bl, 39cr, 50al; J. Allan Cash Photolibrary: 10cl, 13bc, 15al, 23ar, 36ar, 41ar, 41br, 45ar, 56cr, 57ar; Comstock / Simon McBride: 12ar; Geoff Dann: 29ar, 60al; Michael Dent: 62ar; Edifice / Lewis: 10acl, 46cl, 57bcr, 57br / Jackson / Darley: 46ac, 57bl; e.t. archive: 6cl, 17bl, 53ac, 59bc / Victoria and Albert Museum: 11al, 61cl; Chris Fairclough Colour Library: 63cl; Ffotograff / Patricia Aithie: 16ar, 51br, 61al; Sonia Halliday Photographs: 13cr, 34cl, 40c / Jane Taylor: 27ar / F. H. C. Birch: 30br / and Laura Lushington: 50ar, 51al; Robert Harding Picture Library: 7al, 14bc, 27bcr, 30ar, 31al, 62bl / James Strachan: 48bl / Adam Woolfitt: 50cl, 56ar; Michael Holford: 25a, 34bl, 61br; Angelo Hornak Library: 7br, 10ar, 12cr, 31ar; Hulton Deutsch Collection Ltd: 62br; Hutchison Library / Victoria Southwell: 12bcl; Nancy Durrell McKenna: 36al / Julia Davey: 38bc; The Image Bank / Wilkes: 15tr / Weinberg / Clark: 22ar / Bernard Van Berg: 27bl / Peter Holst: 29al / Guido Alberto Rossi: 29ac / Andrea Pistolesi: 33br, 39al / Romilly Lockyer: 41bl

/ Michael Coyne: 63al; Images Colour Library Ltd: 24br; Junckers / Sheila Fitzjones Associates, PR Consultancy: 45cr, 45br; A. F. Kersting: 10-11b; Mansell Collection: 14cl; James H. Morris: 12acl, 13cl, 22c, 44ac, 48cl, 55ac, 57al; Pictor International, London: 6bl, 53ar, 63ac; Royal Geographical Society / Chris Caldicott: 11acl; Tony Stone Images: 26al / Robin Smith: 7ar / Charlie Waite: 27br / Hugh Sitton: 38bl / Thierry Cazabon: 62cr; Wim Swaan: 50bl; Syndication International / Trinity College, Dublin: 17ar; Travel Photo International: 10bl; Trip / Helene Rogers: 17cr, 51bc, 60bl, 63r / George Heath: 41cr; Wurttembergische Landesbibliothek, Stuttgart (Cod.Bibl.2 / 5, fol 9v) / Photo: Baumgardt Grossfotos: 6ar; Zefa Picture Library (UK) Ltd: 7acr, 11ar, 13ar, 14bl, 28al, 28ar, 29acl, 31br, 46bl, 46br, 56bl, 56br, 59br

Every effort has been made to trace the copyright holders and we apologize in advance for any unintentional omissions. We would be pleased to insert the appropriate acknowledgment in any subsequent edition of this publication.

1 BIRD
2 ROCKS & MINERALS
3 SKELETON
4 ARMS & ARMOR
5 TREE
6 POND & RIVER
7 BUTTERFLY & MOTH
8 SPORTS
9 SHELL
10 EARLY HUMANS
11 MAMMAL
12 MUSIC
13 DINOSAUR
14 PLANT
15 SEASHORE
16 FLAG
17 INSECT
18 MONEY
19 FOSSIL
20 FISH
21 CAR
22 FLYING MACHINE
23 ANCIENT EGYPT
24 ANCIENT ROME
25 CRYSTAL & GEM
26 REPTILE
27 INVENTION
28 WEATHER
29 CAT
30 BIBLE LANDS
31 EXPLORER
32 DOG
33 HORSE
34 FILM
35 COSTUME
36 BOAT
37 ANCIENT GREECE
38 VOLCANO & EARTHQUAKE
39 TRAIN
40 SHARK
41 AMPHIBIAN
42 ELEPHANT
43 KNIGHT
44 MUMMY
45 COWBOY
46 WHALE
47 AZTEC, INCA & MAYA
48 BOOK
49 CASTLE
50 VIKING
51 DESERT
52 PREHISTORIC LIFE
53 PYRAMID
54 JUNGLE
55 ANCIENT CHINA
56 ARCHEOLOGY
57 ARCTIC & ANTARCTIC
58 BUILDING
59 PIRATE
60 NORTH AMERICAN INDIAN
61 AFRICA
62 OCEAN
63 BATTLE
64 GORILLA, MONKEY & APE
65 MEDIEVAL LIFE
66 FARM
67 SPY
68 RELIGION
69 EAGLE & BIRDS OF PREY
70 WITCHES & MAGIC-MAKERS
71 SPACE EXPLORATION
72 SHIPWRECK